T0298774

IoT, Machine Learning and Data Analytics for Smart Healthcare

Machine learning, Internet of Things (IoT) and data analytics are new and fresh technologies that are being increasingly adopted in the field of medicine. This book positions itself at the forefront of this movement, exploring the beneficial applications of these new technologies and how they are gradually creating a smart healthcare system.

This book details the various ways in which machine learning, data analytics and IoT solutions are instrumental in disease prediction in smart healthcare. For example, wearable sensors further help doctors and healthcare managers to monitor patients remotely and collect their health parameters in real-time, which can then be used to create datasets to develop machine learning models that can aid in the prediction and detection of any susceptible disease. In this way, smart healthcare can provide novel solutions to traditional medical issues.

This book is a useful overview for scientists, researchers, practitioners and academics specialising in the field of intelligent healthcare, as well as containing additional appeal as a reference book for undergraduate and graduate students.

IoT, Machine Learning and Data Analytics for Smart Healthcare

Edited by
Mourade Azrour, Jamal Mabrouki, Azidine Guezzaz,
Sultan Ahmad, Shakir Khan and Said Benkirane

CRC Press
Taylor & Francis Group
Boca Raton London New York

CRC Press is an imprint of the
Taylor & Francis Group, an **informa** business

Designed cover image: Mourade Azrour

First edition published 2024
by CRC Press
2385 NW Executive Center Drive, Suite 320, Boca Raton FL 33431

and by CRC Press
4 Park Square, Milton Park, Abingdon, Oxon, OX14 4RN

CRC Press is an imprint of Taylor & Francis Group, LLC

ISBN: 9781032551074 (hbk)
ISBN: 9781032724362 (pbk)
ISBN: 9781003430735 (ebk)

DOI: 10.1201/9781003430735

Typeset in Minion
by Newgen Publishing UK

To my dear little daughter AZROUR Israe;
I hope that you will have tomorrow what you don't have today.

Contents

Editor Biographies, ix

List of Contributors, xiii

CHAPTER 1 ▪ Applications of Blockchain in Healthcare: Review Study   1

SOUHAYLA DARGAOUI, MOURADE AZROUR, AHMAD EL ALLAOUI, AZIDINE GUEZZAZ, SAID BENKIRANE, ABDULATIF ALABDULATIF AND FATIMA AMOUNAS

CHAPTER 2 ▪ Deep Learning for Healthcare Management   13

ANKUSH VERMA, AMIT PRATAP SINGH CHOUHAN, VANDANA SINGH, SANJANA KORANGA AND MOURADE AZROUR

CHAPTER 3 ▪ Exploring Lung Cancer Pathologies Using Metaphoric Interventions of Deep Learning Techniques   25

SWAPNALI PATIL AND D. LAKSHMI

CHAPTER 4 ▪ Artificial Intelligence in Smart Healthcare   42

ANKUSH VERMA, ANAM MOHAMED SALEEM, JOYCE PRABHUDAS RANADIVE, AMIT PRATAP SINGH CHOUHAN AND VANDANA SINGH

CHAPTER 5 ▪ Biometrics and Data Smart Healthcare System   57

ANKUSH VERMA, ANAM MOHAMED SALEEM, JOYCE PRABHUDAS RANADIVE, AMIT PRATAP SINGH CHOUHAN AND VANDANA SINGH

CHAPTER 6 ▪ Analysing the Ascendant Trend of Veganism: A Comprehensive Study on the Shift towards Sustainable Dietary Choices   71

SHIKHA BHAGAT, SHILPA SARVANI RAVI AND RASHMI RAI

CHAPTER 7 ■ Monitoring of Water Toxicity Through the Internet of Things to Protect the Health of the Population   85

KHADIJA EL-MOUSTAQIM, JAMAL MABROUKI AND MOURADE AZROUR

INDEX, 93

Editor Biographies

Mourade Azrour received his PhD from the Faculty of Sciences and Techniques, Moulay Ismail University of Meknès, Morocco. He received his MS in computer and distributed systems from the Faculty of Sciences, Ibn Zouhr University, Agadir, Morocco in 2014. Mourade currently works as a computer sciences professor at the Department of Computer Science, Faculty of Sciences and Techniques, Moulay Ismail University of Meknès. His research interests include authentication protocol, computer security, the Internet of Things, smart systems and machine learning. Mourade is a member of the scientific committees of numerous international conferences. He is also a reviewer of various scientific journals. He has published more than 60 scientific papers and book chapters. Mourade has edited 2 scientific books: *IoT and Smart Devices for Sustainable Environment* (2022) and *Advanced Technology for Smart Environment and Energy* (2023). Finally, he has served as guest editor of the journals *EAI Endorsed Transactions on Internet of Things*, *Tsinghua Science and Technology*, *Applied Sciences MDPI* and *Sustainability MDPI*.

Jamal Mabrouki received his PhD in process and environmental engineering at Mohammed V University in Rabat, specializing in artificial intelligence and smart automatic systems. He completed the Bachelor of Science in physics and chemistry with honors from Hassan II University in Casablanca, Morocco. His research is on intelligent monitoring, control, and management systems and more particularly on sensing and supervising remote intoxication systems, smart self-supervised systems and recurrent neural networks. He has published several papers in conferences and indexed journals, most of them related to artificial intelligent systems, the Internet of Things or big data and mining. Jamal currently works as a professor in environment, energy and smart systems in the Faculty of Science, Mohammed V University in Rabat. Jamal is a scientific committee member of numerous national and international conferences. He is also a reviewer of *Modeling Earth Systems and Environment*; *International Journal of Environmental Analytical Chemistry*; *International Journal of Modeling, Simulation, and Scientific Computing*; *The Journal of Supercomputing, Energy & Environment*; and *Big Data Mining and Analytics*, among others.

Azidine Guezzaz received his PhD from Ibn Zohr University Agadir, Morocco in 2018. He obtained his master's in computer and distributed systems from the Faculty of Sciences, Ibn Zouhr University, Agadir, Morocco in 2013. He is currently an associate professor of computer science and mathematics at Cadi Ayyad University Marrakech, Morocco. His main research interests are computer security, cryptography, artificial intelligence, intrusion detection and smart cities. He is a member of the scientific and organizing committees of various international conferences. Azidine is a guest editor of special issues of *Tsinghua Science and Technology*, *Sustainability* and *EAI Endorsed Transactions on Internet of Things*. He is also an editor of some books and a reviewer of various scientific journals.

Sultan Ahmad is an IEEE Member. He received his PhD from Glocal University and a Master's in Computer Science and Applications from the prestigious Aligarh Muslim University, India with distinction marks. Presently, he is working as faculty in the Department of Computer Science, College of Computer Engineering and Sciences, Prince Sattam Bin Abdulaziz University, Alkharj, Saudi Arabia. He is also Adjunct Professor at Chandigarh University, Gharuan, Punjab, India. He has more than 15 years of teaching and research experience. He has around 80 accepted and published research papers and book chapters in reputed SCI, SCIE, ESCI and SCOPUS-indexed journals and conferences. He has an Australian patent in his name also. He has authored 4 books that are available on Amazon. His research areas include distributed computing, big data, machine learning and the Internet of Things. He has presented his research papers at many national and international conferences. He is a Member of IEEE, IACSIT and the Computer Society of India.

Shakir Khan has a PhD in computer science and is a senior member of IEEE, presently working as an associate professor in the College of Computer and Information Sciences (CCIS), Imam Mohammad Ibn Saud Islamic University (IMSIU), Riyadh, Saudi Arabia. He has more than 15 years of rich national and international teaching, research and IT experience, including five years in King Saud University for research, training and teaching, Riyadh, Saudi Arabia. He has sound research knowledge along with supervision of more than a dozen master's level scholars in different fields of computer science. He has published more than 90 articles in reputed journals and conferences. He has also published three books and has three patents. He has contributed to many international journals and conferences as editor, member of the advisory board, reviewer, program committee member and keynote speaker. His research interests include data mining, data science, AI, cloud computing, IoT, big data and analytics, bioinformatics, E-learning, machine learning and deep learning. He received a research excellence award from Imam University in 2019, and led the programming team at Prince Sultan University, Riyadh, who came third out of 40 national teams from different Saudi universities. He has been awarded multiple research grants from Deanship of Scientific Research, Imam University and the Ministry of Education, Saudi Arabia. He is the PI for the International Research Partnership Program with one of the computer science professors in Aligarh Muslim University (AMU), India. Dr. Khan is delivering these projects and is also doing collaborative research with the University of Electronic Science and Technology China (UESTC), and other professors globally.

Said Benkirane obtained his engineering degree in networks and telecommunications in 2004 from INPT in Rabat, Morocco. He obtained his master's degree in computer and network engineering in 2006 from the USMBA University of Fez and his PhD in computer science in 2013 from the UCD University of El-Jadida, Morocco. He has been working as a professor at ESTE Cadi Ayyad University since 2014. His areas of research are artificial intelligence, multi agents and systems security. He also works in various wireless networks. He is president of the Robotics and Artificial Intelligence Team; he is also an active reviewer in several high-quality journals.

Contributors

Abdulatif Alabdulatif
Department of Computer Science, College of Computer, Qassim University, Buraydah, Saudi Arabia

Ahmad El Allaoui
STI Laboratory, IDMS Team, Faculty of Sciences and Techniques, Moulay Ismail University of Meknes, Errachidia, Morocco

Fatima Amounas
Computer Science Department, Faculty of Sciences and Techniques, Moulay Ismail University of Meknes, Errachidia, Morocco

Mourade Azrour
STI Laboratory, IDMS Team, Faculty of Sciences and Techniques, Moulay Ismail University of Meknes, Errachidia, Morocco

Said Benkirane
Higher School Essaouira, Cadi Ayyad University, Morocco

Shikha Bhagat
School of Business and Management, Christ University, India

Amit Pratap Singh Chouhan
Department of Radiology, Sharda School of Allied Health Sciences, Sharda University, Greater Noida, U.P., India

D. Lakshmi
VIT Bhopal University, Madhya Pradesh, India

Souhayla Dargaoui
STI Laboratory, IDMS Team, Faculty of Sciences and Techniques, Moulay Ismail University of Meknes, Errachidia, Morocco

Khadija El-Moustaqim
Faculty of sciences, Mohammed V University in Rabat, Morocco

Azidine Guezzaz
Higher School Essaouira, Cadi Ayyad University, Morocco

Sanjana Koranga
Department of Anatomy, Sharda School of Allied Health Sciences, Sharda University, Greater Noida, U.P., India

Jamal Mabrouki
Laboratory of Spectroscopy, Molecular Modelling, Materials, Nanomaterial,

Water and Environment, CERNE2D,
Mohammed V, University in Rabat,
Faculty of Science, Avenue Ibn Battouta,
Agdal, Rabat, Morocco

Swapnali Patil
VIT Bhopal University, Madhya
Pradesh, India

Rashmi Rai
School of Business and Management,
Christ University, India

Joyce Prabhudas Ranadive
Department of Nursing, Sharda School of
Nursing Science and Research, Sharda
University, Greater Noida, U.P., India

Shilpa Sarvani Ravi
School of Business and Management,
Christ University, India

Anam Mohamed Saleem
Department of Nursing, Sharda School of
Nursing Science and Research, Sharda
University, Greater Noida, U.P., India

Vandana Singh
Department of Microbiology, Sharda
School of Allied Health Sciences,
Sharda University, Greater Noida,
U.P., India

Ankush Verma
Department of Radiology, Sharda School
of Allied Health Sciences, Sharda
University, Greater Noida, U.P., India

CHAPTER 1

Applications of Blockchain in Healthcare: Review Study

Souhayla Dargaoui, Mourade Azrour, Ahmad
El Allaoui, Azidine Guezzaz, Said Benkirane,
Abdulatif Alabdulatif and Fatima Amounas

1.1 INTRODUCTION

The healthcare field constitutes one of the fundamental areas of activity that has a major impact on the international community as a whole and is intimately associated with each country's level of development. In addition, this sector makes a major contribution to maintaining and consolidating national economic stability. As a result, healthcare services are at the heart of government policies worldwide, especially after the spread of the coronavirus in 2019.

The efficient and safe management and gathering of the enormous volumes of patient health data produced by routine operations and service activities represents a significant challenge for medical professionals[1]. In addition, medical monitoring systems based on Internet of Things (IoT)[2]–[6], including handheld equipment, are generating considerable volumes of private health data[7]–[10]. Such data are usually not accessible, are not standardized, and are not easy to comprehend, deploy and share. Furthermore, these data are sourced from numerous different sources and stored in centralized systems, which makes their management and exchange extremely difficult.

Blockchain is a particularly attractive research topic, and various disciplines have been exploiting its advantages in the last few years[11]–[13]. Thus, academics, designers and professionals have conceived an increasingly strong and powerful enthusiasm. Accordingly, new structures, new systems and multiple projects have emerged. The Bitcoin, the Ethereum and Hyperledger are at the forefront of those developments, which have all contributed to a variety of issues relating to the deployment of blockchain. In healthcare, adopting blockchain technology could offer a wide range of advantages, including improved security[3], [5], [14]–[17], stronger respect for privacy, more confidentiality and more decentralization solutions.

The studies published to date[18]–[27] present brief overviews of the most recent developments in blockchain-based healthcare, and highlight both the advantages and disadvantages of the various solutions proposed by researchers. The aim of this research is to conduct an in-depth study of the available literature and identify the opportunities offered by blockchain applications in various healthcare services. It also examines research directions, challenges and future research directions in the field of blockchain-based healthcare systems.

The remainder of this chapter is organized as follows. In section two, we give some background information about traditional healthcare systems and blockchain. In section three, published related works are presented. In section four, we describe the research methodology adopted in this chapter. Section five is reserved for presenting the obtained results and their discussions. The last section concludes the chapter.

1.2 BACKGROUND

1.2.1 Traditional Healthcare Systems

Health data processing is a fundamental element in safeguarding and processing patient registers to provide more effective care, efficiently tracking pathologies and their origins, providing sufficient medical data for research purposes, development of new and more effective drugs, and finally enabling an adequate prevention system to be put in place. Hospitals and healthcare organizations currently use local management applications to manage patient medical data, based on client-server architecture. However, these applications do not share data between them, making it difficult to establish an accurate diagnosis when professionals and patients need to have a coherent view of their medical history. To overcome this problem, cloud-based applications have been designed by researchers and industries alike. While these applications allow patients to store important medical records in a cloud database, they also pose problems of security, data loss and privacy[28]–[31].

1.2.2 Blockchain

The concept of blockchain first came to prominence with Satoshi Nakamoto, creator of Bitcoin, the very first crypto-currency[19]. Blockchain is a technology for storing and at the same time transmitting transactions. It enables a set of blocks of data to be stored within the transaction register. Each block is associated with its predecessors to build up a series of blocks. In this context, a peer-to-peer network guarantees the communication of information. Blockchain technology therefore refers to the distributed ledger, which is shared securely and decentralized. Over the past few years, blockchain has experienced extraordinary growth across the financial and banking sectors. It is now making its way into other fields like assurance, energy, industry and healthcare. Hence, blockchain can be used in various applications such as online voting systems, e-commerce shopping, social networks, e-games, messaging, and e-learning. As a result, blockchain is gaining in popularity in virtually every sector, thanks to its decentralized, distributed and secure characteristics. Indeed, as the system is decentralized, it does not require a central administration to govern it. Data storage is based on a process of mutual agreement between the various nodes, using a consensus algorithm. Blockchain provides an answer to the problems posed by different solutions for centrally securing the rescue and sharing of data in cloud computing.

1.3 RELATED WORK

Blockchain is a crucial invention that has a significant purpose in today's commerce world. It refers to a digital record of repetitious transactions diffused throughout a network. It may be used as a storage and sharing data system that is difficult to be altered or hacked. Recently, blockchain technology has been widely used in several domains; one of the most attractive fields to use this technology is healthcare. Regarding the application situations there are three types of blockchain use cases in smart healthcare systems. The recording and security of data are the first type. The second one is the combination of IoMT with blockchain. The third option is to use blockchain instead of the central institution of federal learning. In the last few years, so many review studies of blockchain applications in healthcare have been published. In [23] Pranto Kumar Ghosh et al. provided a review of the current papers that consider the applications of blockchain technology in the healthcare industry. The review summarizes 144 research papers that illustrate the significance and highlight the limitations of this technology in this field. At first, the authors present an exhaustive background of blockchain and its characteristics. Then they focus on affording the literature survey of the nominated papers that highlight the present themes in blockchain-enabled smart healthcare. Additionally, they present the solutions offered by the blockchain in several application zones. Finally, the authors present the issues and future research directions.

Similarly, Sadia Ramzan [32] et al. presented an overview of blockchain-based healthcare. Firstly, an extensive introduction, history, background, and blockchain kinds were presented. Then, this technology's motivations and healthcare services completed using it have been covered. The paper demonstrates the potency of blockchain, identifies its challenges and highlights future research directions. To examine recent research in this domain Valeria Merlo et al. also provided a review that focuses on blockchain utilizations in real situations[33]. They prove that the open research issues are data security and the realization of electronic health records and diagnosis systems.

Suruchi Singh et al. afford a review[34] that explains how blockchain technology may boost medical record administrations and maintain the integrity and privacy of patient's data. They presented a wide range of applications using this technology, highlighting its implementation benefits, especially in healthcare data management. Then they discuss various remarkable challenges which tardy this techno approbation in such domains. Eventually, they suggested numerous other points for examination. In [35] Mohammad Salar Arbabi et al. give an in-depth overview of the state of blockchain-enabled healthcare solutions using a framework for systems classification and analysis. The authors examine over 40 provided solutions and categorize each one based on functional components, advantages, and issues. There is so much research that reviews the recent development of blockchain-based healthcare solutions[36]–[40].

1.4 RESEARCH METHODOLOGY

In this section, we outline the steps (Figure 1.1) followed to collect the literature required in the present survey.

As the first process in the review study, we determined three questions to be resolved in this study, in line with the goal to be achieved, which is to determine the state of research on blockchain technology applications in healthcare services. Accordingly, the questions employed to identify articles appropriate to the aims of this study are as follows:

- What are the latest published works that deal with the application of blockchain on the healthcare subject?
- What are the different purposes of blockchain applications in healthcare management?
- What are the challenges and issues of blockchain applications in healthcare management?

With a view to producing ideal search queries, a number of measures have been suggested in[41]–[43] to subdivide search queries, namely by distinguishing certain criteria, including search groupings, abbreviations and variant spellings, which are combined by means of Boolean operators.

The various steps involved in achieving the final result of the process line are outlined in the following sections:

- Select the abstract and related words within the paper identified in the first search.
- Building search queries based on logic operators such as "OR," "AND," or "NOT."
- Find keywords, terms, abbreviations and synonyms.

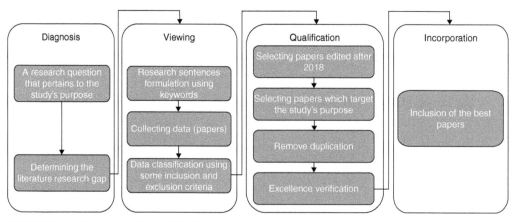

FIGURE 1.1   The steps followed for literature review.

Thanks to the elaborate search sequence, significant research articles were examined. To achieve this goal, we only consulted the main databases containing scientific publications, such as IEEE XPLORE, Science Direct, Springer, Taylor & Francis and MDPI. Taking these different sources as our starting point, we selected 15 research documents in particular.

1.5 RESULTS AND DISCUSSIONS

- What are the latest published works that deal with the application of blockchain on the healthcare subject?
- What are the different purposes of blockchain applications in healthcare management?

In this sub-section, we discuss the reasons that encourage blockchain usage for data management in the healthcare field; as well, we present various purposes of blockchain applications in this domain.

Nowadays, many aspects support the use of blockchain technology in data management. First of all, thanks to IoT, and in particular Internet of Medical Things (IoMT), equipment essentially collects information via sensors[44]. So, there has been an exponential increase in the number of sensors, opening the way to the creation of global sensor networks requiring a new, high-performance data management system[45]. What's more, this infrastructure instantaneously produces highly heterogeneous datasets, leading to the development of what is known as Big Data. Nevertheless, conventional data processing approaches are insufficiently adaptable to handle the huge volumes of data, requiring the development of a more rigorous data processing system. Finally, legacy data management tools based on client/server exchanges, which are now employed in the healthcare and IoT sectors, are vulnerable to occasional failures. In addition, the architectures, protocols and procedures of distributed networks are unable to cope with new constraints and meet constantly changing service expectations. Furthermore, information stored on different servers is frequently unencrypted, posing a real security risk, whereas blockchain-based systems employ data storage mechanisms using multiple encryption modes. Finally, in the case of IoT-enabled systems, both online and offline transactions are carried out, which traditional data management methods find difficult to address[46]. Consequently, it was necessary to design a new data management model capable of guaranteeing data communication in small packets, which does not require high bandwidth.

1.5.1 Patient Data Storage

Patient data refers to the content of a given patient's medical records. Such data may include information relating to past and present health or illness, treatment history, lifestyle habits and genetic characteristics[47]. It may also include biometric data, i.e. any physical characteristic that can be measured by a machine or computer. Therefore, the volume of privately generated data increases day after day, making their storage in a secure manner a new issue. Hence, healthcare providers resort to the usage of blockchain. In addition, blockchain is capable of building a reliable and secure storage infrastructure. Medical archive records management is simply the basic process of adding, deleting, modifying and querying. Nevertheless, with blockchain, the two core archival information processing operations of deleting and modifying are no longer necessary, reducing the amount of information that needs to be processed. The technical design of the blockchain provides assurances of irreparability and data security. Furthermore, within blockchain, each information block registers the creation time and the previous block's hash value[48].

1.5.2 Medical Image Sharing

Sharing medical images involves the electronic exchange of medical images between hospitals, doctors' practices and patient groups. Contrary to traditional media, notably CDs or DVDs, that patients either carry around with them or receive by post, the new technology currently facilitates the exchange of these images via cloud computing[49].

Sharing images thanks to the blockchain is possible either through public sharing or through private sharing. In a public blockchain, the transaction details of a patient are added to the blockchain, allowing other healthcare systems to visualize that patient's medical images[50]. However, in a private blockchain, individual members as well as organized groups can be authorized to consult a patient's medical images. With blockchain, transactions between providers are carried out independently of any third party. Allowing healthcare providers and patients respectively to transfer and upload their data using the blockchain network, every member has access to a universally accessible, secure, real-time dataset. The blockchain delivers a collaborative disease diagnosis solution, with full access to all medical imaging data available for a patient[51]–[53]. This can definitely allow more accurate detection and improved treatment of diseases[54].

1.5.3 Patient Monitoring

Blockchain technology gives medical service managers access to equipment tailored to their needs[55]–[57]. At the same time, doctors are likely to spend more time monitoring patient progress and intervening remotely when any health-related issues arise. Blockchain technology and the healthcare system offer the possibility of monitoring temperature conditions at any time of the day, as well as checking bed utilization and the correct availability of medication. Blockchain maintains a healthcare service network that aims to implement consistent digital identification for healthcare organizations and healthcare service providers. The combination of blockchain and IoT technologies improves the speed of response and transparency of the supply chain, enabling healthcare logistics to run more smoothly and ensure effective patient monitoring[58], [59].

- What are the challenges and issues of blockchain applications in healthcare management?

Blockchain technology is being integrated into the healthcare sector, for which particular difficulties would have to be taken into account. The main obstacle to the implementation of this advanced technology by medical structures lies in the lack of **expertise**. Indeed, the development of blockchain applications is still very recent and researching and implementing new technologies requires considerable effort. However, this system is applicable to medical organizations as well as to the requirements of supervisory authorities. Therefore, medicine and healthcare is likely to be faced with **standardization** problems. International standards authorities would certainly need to provide a certain set of well-authenticated and certified standards. The time has come for the healthcare sector to make improvements. It is highly likely that the use of blockchain will become widespread in the healthcare world in the future. This techno-logical innovation will contribute to the growth of healthcare applications, not least by making it easier to explain the effects and progress of treatment protocol. Indeed, blockchain technology is essential for confirming **transactions and information transfers**.

Managing **storage** capacity is one of the challenges facing the use of blockchain. Indeed, blockchain was initially specified for storing and exploiting transaction data, which is

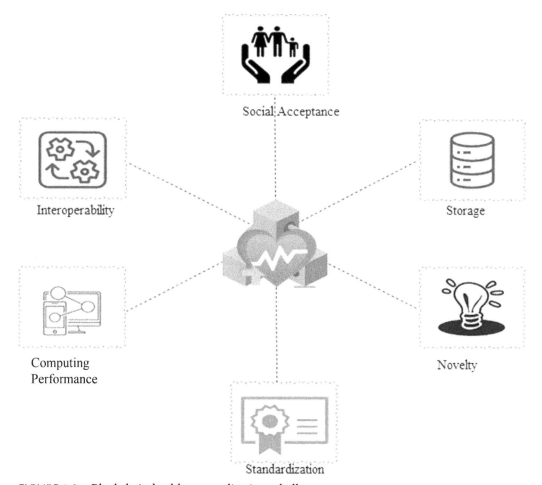

FIGURE 1.2   Blockchain healthcare applications challenges.

restricted in scope, so that its storage does not require a large amount of data. However, as it expanded into healthcare services, storage issues obviously appeared.

Blockchain is experiencing challenges related to **interoperability**, in other words, it is difficult to enable various blockchain-based applications designed with different operators or service providers to communicate with each other in a transparent and appropriate way. Hence, this challenge affects data exchange capability.

Blockchain technology is still evolving and therefore faces **social challenges**, including cultural challenges, in addition to the technical challenges mentioned above. Indeed, a technology that is totally distinct from old ways of working can never be easily accepted and adopted. Even if the medical sector is gradually moving towards digitization, there is still a long way to go before it can fully adopt this technology, especially when it comes to a technology like blockchain, on which clinical criteria are not yet valid.

1.6 CONCLUSION AND FUTURE WORK

Nowadays, the healthcare domain knows a great evolution. In fact, it takes advantage of recently developed technologies like IoT, Machine Learning, blockchain and so on. Hence, the medical services offer doctors and medical service providers the ability to follow easily patients remotely and in real time. The deployment of such technologies generates high and various patient data that must be stored and shared securely. Subsequently, the present chapter highlights different applications of blockchain in the healthcare field as it presents some advantages and challenges of this technology.

REFERENCES

[1]   A. Clim, R. D. Zota, and G. Tinica, "Big Data in home healthcare: A new frontier in personalized medicine. Medical emergency services and prediction of hypertension risks," *International Journal of Healthcare Management*, vol. 12, no. 3, pp. 241–249, 2019.

[2]   M. Azrour, M. Ouanan, Y. Farhaoui, and A. Guezzaz, "Security analysis of Ye et al. authentication protocol for Internet of Things," in *Big Data and Smart Digital Environment*, Springer, 2019, pp. 67–74.

[3]   C. Hazman, A. Guezzaz, S. Benkirane, and M. Azrour, "lIDS-SIoEL: Intrusion detection framework for IoT-based smart environments security using ensemble learning," *Cluster Computing*, vol. 26, pp. 4069–4083, 2023.

[4]   M. Douiba, S. Benkirane, A. Guezzaz, and M. Azrour, "Anomaly detection model based on gradient boosting and decision tree for IoT environments security," *Journal of Reliable Intelligent Environments*, pp. 1–12, 2022. https://doi.org/10.1007/s40860-022-00184-3

[5]   A. Guezzaz, M. Azrour, S. Benkirane, M. Mohyeddine, H. Attou, and M. Douiba, "A lightweight hybrid intrusion detection framework using machine learning for Edge-Based IIoT security," *International Arab Journal of Information Technology*, vol. 19, no. 5, pp. 822–830, 2022.

[6]   M. Douiba, S. Benkirane, A. Guezzaz, and M. Azrour, "An improved anomaly detection model for IoT security using decision tree and gradient boosting," *Journal of Supercomputing*, pp. 1–20, 2022.

[7]   F. Subhan *et al.*, "AI-Enabled wearable medical internet of things in healthcare system: A survey," *Applied Sciences*, vol. 13, no. 3, pp. 1394, 2023.

[8] N. Y. Philip, J. J. Rodrigues, H. Wang, S. J. Fong, and J. Chen, "Internet of Things for in-home health monitoring systems: Current advances, challenges and future directions," *IEEE Journal on Selected Areas in Communications*, vol. 39, no. 2, pp. 300–310, 2021.

[9] H. H. Alshammari, "The internet of things healthcare monitoring system based on MQTT protocol," *Alexandria Engineering Journal*, vol. 69, pp. 275–287, 2023.

[10] J. Srivastava, S. Routray, S. Ahmad, and M. M. Waris, "Internet of medical things (IoMT)-based smart healthcare system: Trends and progress," *Computational Intelligence and Neuroscience*, vol. 2022, pp. 1–17, 2022.

[11] N. M. Kumar and P. K. Mallick, "Blockchain technology for security issues and challenges in IoT," *Procedia Computer Science*, vol. 132, pp. 1815–1823, 2018.

[12] D. Miller, "Blockchain and the internet of things in the industrial sector," *IT Professional*, vol. 20, no. 3, pp. 15–18, 2018.

[13] M. Di Pierro, "What is the blockchain?," *Computing in Science & Engineering*, vol. 19, no. 5, pp. 92–95, 2017.

[14] C. Hazman, S. Benkirane, A. Guezzaz, M. Azrour, and M. Abdedaime, "Intrusion detection framework for IoT-Based smart environments security," in *Artificial Intelligence and Smart Environment: ICAISE'2022*, Springer, 2023, pp. 546–552.

[15] M. Azrour, M. Ouanan, and Y. Farhaoui, "SIP authentication protocols based on elliptic curve cryptography: Survey and comparison," *Indonesian Journal of Electrical Engineering and Computer Science*, vol. 4, no. 1, pp. 231, Oct. 2016. DOI: 10.11591/ijeecs.v4.i1.pp231-239

[16] A. Guezzaz, S. Benkirane, and M. Azrour, "A Novel anomaly network intrusion detection system for internet of things security," in *IoT and Smart Devices for Sustainable Environment*, Springer, 2022, pp. 129–138.

[17] S. Dargaoui *et al.*, "An overview of the security challenges in IoT environment," in *Advanced Technology for Smart Environment and Energy*, J. Mabrouki, A. Mourade, A. Irshad, and S. A. Chaudhry, Eds., in Environmental Science and Engineering. Cham: Springer International Publishing, 2023, pp. 151–160. DOI: 10.1007/978-3-031-25662-2_13

[18] M. AlShamsi, M. Al-Emran, and K. Shaalan, "A systematic review on blockchain adoption," *Applied Sciences*, vol. 12, no. 9, pp. 4245, 2022.

[19] A.-I. Florea, I. Anghel, and T. Cioara, "A review of blockchain technology applications in ambient assisted living," *Future Internet*, vol. 14, no. 5, pp. 150, 2022.

[20] A. H. Mayer, C. A. da Costa, and R. da R. Righi, "Electronic health records in a blockchain: A systematic review," *Health Informatics Journal*, vol. 26, no. 2, pp. 1273–1288, 2020.

[21] I. Abu-Elezz, A. Hassan, A. Nazeemudeen, M. Househ, and A. Abd-Alrazaq, "The benefits and threats of blockchain technology in healthcare: A scoping review," *International Journal of Medical Informatics*, vol. 142, pp. 104246, 2020.

[22] C. C. Agbo, Q. H. Mahmoud, and J. M. Eklund, "Blockchain technology in healthcare: A systematic review," *Healthcare*, vol. 7, no. 2, Jun. 2019. DOI: 10.3390/healthcare7020056

[23] P. K. Ghosh, A. Chakraborty, M. Hasan, K. Rashid, and A. H. Siddique, "Blockchain application in healthcare systems: A Review," *Systems*, vol. 11, no. 1, Jan. 2023. DOI: 10.3390/systems11010038

[24] E. J. De Aguiar, B. S. Faiçal, B. Krishnamachari, and J. Ueyama, "A Survey of blockchain-based strategies for healthcare," *ACM Computing Surveys*, vol. 53, no. 2, pp. 27:1–27:27, Mar. 2020. DOI: 10.1145/3376915

[25] M. Hölbl, M. Kompara, A. Kamišalić, and L. Nemec Zlatolas, "A systematic review of the use of blockchain in healthcare," *Symmetry*, vol. 10, no. 10, Oct. 2018. DOI: 10.3390/sym10100470

[26] M. Attaran, "Blockchain technology in healthcare: Challenges and opportunities," *International Journal of Healthcare Management*, vol. 15, no. 1, pp. 70–83, Jan. 2022. DOI: 10.1080/20479700.2020.1843887

[27] E. M. Adere, "Blockchain in healthcare and IoT: A systematic literature review," *Array*, vol. 14, pp. 100139, Jul. 2022. DOI: 10.1016/j.array.2022.100139

[28] K. Abouelmehdi, A. Beni-Hessane, and H. Khaloufi, "Big healthcare data: Preserving security and privacy," *Journal of Big Data*, vol. 5, no. 1, pp. 1–18, 2018.

[29] M. Azrour, J. Mabrouki, and R. Chaganti, "New efficient and secured authentication protocol for remote healthcare systems in Cloud-IoT," *Security and Communication Networks*, vol. 2021, pp. 1–12, May 2021. DOI: 10.1155/2021/5546334

[30] R. Chaganti, M. Azrour, R. Vinayakumar, V. Naga, A. Dua, and B. Bhushan, "A particle swarm optimization and deep learning approach for intrusion detection system in internet of medical things." *Sustainability*, vol. 14, pp. 12828, 2022.

[31] M. Azrour and J. Mabrouki, "Data analytics to assess the outbreak of the coronavirus epidemic: Opportunities and challenges," in *Intelligent Modeling, Prediction, and Diagnosis from Epidemiological Data*, 1st ed. Boca Raton: Chapman and Hall/CRC, 2021, pp. 47–62. DOI: 10.1201/9781003158684-3

[32] S. Ramzan, A. Aqdus, V. Ravi, D. Koundal, R. Amin, and M. A. Al Ghamdi, "Healthcare applications using blockchain technology: Motivations and challenges," *IEEE Transactions on Engineering Management*, pp. 2874–2890, 2022.

[33] V. Merlo, G. Pio, F. Giusto, and M. Bilancia, "On the exploitation of the blockchain technology in the healthcare sector: A systematic review," *Expert Systems with Applications*, vol. 213, pp. 118897, 2023.

[34] S. Singh, S. K. Sharma, P. Mehrotra, P. Bhatt, and M. Kaurav, "Blockchain technology for efficient data management in healthcare system: Opportunity, challenges and future perspectives," *Materials Today: Proceedings*, vol. 62, pp. 5042–5046, 2022.

[35] M. S. Arbabi, C. Lal, N. R. Veeraragavan, D. Marijan, J. F. Nygård, and R. Vitenberg, "A survey on blockchain for healthcare: Challenges, benefits, and future directions," *IEEE Communications Surveys & Tutorials*, vol. 25, pp. 386–424, 2022.

[36] P. Tagde *et al.*, "Blockchain and artificial intelligence technology in e-Health," *Environmental Science and Pollution Research*, vol. 28, pp. 52810–52831, 2021.

[37] B. Farahani, F. Firouzi, and M. Luecking, "The convergence of IoT and distributed ledger technologies (DLT): Opportunities, challenges, and solutions," *Journal of Network and Computer Applications*, vol. 177, pp. 102936, 2021.

[38] A. Haleem, M. Javaid, R. P. Singh, R. Suman, and S. Rab, "Blockchain technology applications in healthcare: An overview," *International Journal of Intelligent Networks*, vol. 2, pp. 130–139, 2021.

[39] E. Chukwu and L. Garg, "A systematic review of blockchain in healthcare: Frameworks, prototypes, and implementations," *Ieee Access*, vol. 8, pp. 21196–21214, 2020.

[40] A. H. Mayer, C. A. da Costa, and R. da R. Righi, "Electronic health records in a Blockchain: A systematic review," *Health Informatics Journal*, vol. 26, no. 2, pp. 1273–1288, 2020.

[41] J. Khan *et al.*, "Efficient secure surveillance on smart healthcare IoT system through cosine-transform encryption," *Journal of Intelligent & Fuzzy Systems*, vol. 40, no. 1, pp. 1417–1442, 2021.

[42] C. Khan, A. Lewis, E. Rutland, C. Wan, K. Rutter, and C. Thompson, "A distributed-ledger consortium model for collaborative innovation," *Computer*, vol. 50, no. 9, pp. 29–37, 2017.

[43] S. Ahmad *et al.*, "Deep Learning Enabled Disease Diagnosis for Secure Internet of Medical Things," *Computers, Materials & Continua*, vol. 73, no 1, pp. 965–979, 2022.

[44] S. Ahmad, M. Hasan, M. Shahabuddin, T. Tabassum, and M. W. Allvi, "IoT based pill reminder and monitoring system," *International Journal of Computer Science and Network Security*, vol. 20, no. 7, pp. 152–158, 2020.

[45] S. Nazir *et al.*, "A comprehensive analysis of healthcare big data management, analytics and scientific programming," *IEEE Access*, vol. 8, pp. 95714–95733, 2020.

[46] S. Ahmad, A. Alharbi, A. Zamani, and M. Yousufuddin, "Implementation of fusion and filtering techniques in IoT data processing: A case study of smart healthcare," *International Journal of Computer Science and Network Security (IJCSNS)*, vol. 20, no. 12, pp. 131–137, 2020.

[47] M. El Khatib, S. Hamidi, I. Al Ameeri, H. Al Zaabi, and R. Al Marqab, "Digital disruption and big data in healthcare-opportunities and challenges," *ClinicoEconomics and Outcomes Research*, pp. 563–574, 2022.

[48] Z. Sun, D. Han, D. Li, X. Wang, C.-C. Chang, and Z. Wu, "A blockchain-based secure storage scheme for medical information," *EURASIP Journal on Wireless Communications and Networking*, vol. 2022, no. 1, pp. 40, Apr. 2022. DOI: 10.1186/s13638-022-02122-6

[49] M. Adnan, S. Kalra, J. C. Cresswell, G. W. Taylor, and H. R. Tizhoosh, "Federated learning and differential privacy for medical image analysis," *Scientific Reports*, vol. 12, no. 1, pp. 1953, 2022.

[50] R. Xu, S. Chen, L. Yang, Y. Chen, and G. Chen, "Decentralized autonomous imaging data processing using blockchain," in *Multimodal Biomedical Imaging XIV*, SPIE, Feb. 2019, pp. 72–82. DOI: 10.1117/12.2513243

[51] J. Randolph *et al.*, "Blockchain-based medical image sharing and automated critical-results notification: A novel framework," in 2022 IEEE 46th Annual Computers, Software, and Applications Conference (COMPSAC), Los Alamitos, CA, USA: IEEE, Jun. 2022, pp. 1756–1761. DOI: 10.1109/COMPSAC54236.2022.00279.

[52] A. S. Tagliafico *et al.*, "Blockchain in radiology research and clinical practice: Current trends and future directions," *La radiologia medica*, vol. 127, no. 4, pp. 391–397, Apr. 2022. DOI: 10.1007/s11547-022-01460-1

[53] M. P. McBee and C. Wilcox, "Blockchain technology: Principles and applications in medical imaging," *Journal of Digital Imaging*, vol. 33, no. 3, pp. 726–734, Jun. 2020. DOI: 10.1007/s10278-019-00310-3

[54] H. Loukili *et al.*, "Combining multiple regression and principal component analysis to evaluate the effects of ambient air pollution on children's respiratory diseases," *International Journal of Information Tecnology*, vol. 14, no. 3, pp. 1305–1310, May 2022. DOI: 10.1007/s41870-022-00906-z

[55] Yoon, Hyung-Jin, "Blockchain technology and healthcare," *Healthcare Informatics Research*, vol. 25, no 2, pp. 59–60, 2019.

[56] O. Cheikhrouhou, K. Mershad, F. Jamil, R. Mahmud, A. Koubaa, and S. R. Moosavi, "A lightweight blockchain and fog-enabled secure remote patient monitoring system," *Internet of Things*, vol. 22, pp. 100691, 2023.

[57] J. Hathaliya, P. Sharma, S. Tanwar, and R. Gupta, "Blockchain-based remote patient monitoring in healthcare 4.0," in 2019 IEEE 9th *International Conference on Advanced Computing* (IACC), IEEE, 2019, pp. 87–91.

[58] M. J. H. Faruk, H. Shahriar, M. Valero, S. Sneha, S. I. Ahamed, and M. Rahman, "Towards blockchain-based secure data management for remote patient monitoring," in 2021 IEEE *International Conference on Digital Health* (ICDH), IEEE, 2021, pp. 299–308.

[59] P. Mamoshina *et al.*, "Converging blockchain and next-generation artificial intelligence technologies to decentralize and accelerate biomedical research and healthcare," *Oncotarget*, vol. 9, no. 5, pp. 5665–5690, Jan. 2018. DOI: 10.18632/oncotarget.22345

CHAPTER 2

Deep Learning for Healthcare Management

Ankush Verma, Amit Pratap Singh Chouhan, Vandana Singh, Sanjana Koranga and Mourade Azrour

2.1 INTRODUCTION

Artificial intelligence (AI) refers to the intelligence exhibited by machines that simulate human behaviour or thought and that can be programmed and trained specifically for solving certain challenges[1]–[4]. AI is a powerful combination of both machine and deep learning techniques. The AI models are built based on enormous datasets and are able to generate smart decisions. Over the years, artificial intelligence has been applied to a whole variety of domains, such as healthcare[5]–[8], energy[9]–[12], agriculture[13]–[15], security[16]–[20], marketing[21], transportation[22], water management[23]–[27] and so on.

In the healthcare area, AI is rapidly changing the industry by enabling sensing, processing and analysis of large amounts of data in order to improve patient outcomes, reduce costs, and speed up processes. AI is being employed in a range of areas of healthcare administration, from clinical decision-making to administrative tasks. AI is being harnessed to implement high-performance, reliable innovations in the field, which will contribute to the proper management of care provided to patients suffering from so-called chronic diseases, particularly diabetes, cancer, eating disorders or heart disease. Indeed, AI brings many advantages compared to conventional methods when it comes to analysing and making certain clinical decisions. Thanks to AI algorithms, devices become more accurate as training data is assimilated, helping humans to better understand the diversity of treatments, care processes, diagnoses and especially clinical outcomes.

AI is rapidly being applied in healthcare management to improve patient care while lowering expenses. AI systems can analyse vast amounts of data, uncover trends, and generate predictions to assist healthcare providers in making intelligent decisions. Electronic

DOI: 10.1201/9781003430735-2

Health Records (EHRs) are one of the most important applications of AI in healthcare administration. EHRs retain a wealth of patient information that can be leveraged to improve healthcare outcomes[28]. AI systems can mine this data for trends, patterns, and significant health issues. Using AI, it is possible to find and diagnose anomalies in MRI, CT, and X-ray scans as well as analyse medical images. Large volumes of data may be promptly and correctly analysed by AI algorithms to give healthcare professionals insights and recommendations[29]. Healthcare practitioners may also streamline administrative activities like appointment scheduling, billing, and insurance claims management with the aid of AI-powered virtual assistants and chatbots. Because of this, healthcare professionals may devote more time to caring for patients. Through its assistance in the creation of individualised treatment regimens for patients, AI can also enhance patient outcomes. AI algorithms can determine which medicines are most successful for certain patients by analysing patient data, which lowers the possibility of side effects[30]. As a result, the way healthcare is provided is being revolutionised by the application of AI in management. By improving patient outcomes, lowering costs, and increasing efficiency, AI is supporting healthcare professionals in providing better care to more people.

This chapter addresses the numerous applications of artificial intelligence in healthcare administration, as well as its benefits and limitations. Hence, the remainder of this chapter is organised as follows: In section two, we describe some applications of AI in healthcare management as well as the advantages and limits of those applications. Ethical considerations in artificial intelligence for healthcare management are detailed in section three. In section four, some future AI in healthcare management is listed. Section five presents particular successful implementation of AI in healthcare management. The last section concludes the chapter.

2.2 APPLICATIONS OF AI IN HEALTHCARE MANAGEMENT

In the healthcare field, machine learning is most commonly exploited for precision medicine. The latter aims to determine the type of care that will give the best results with a certain number of patients, based on previously collected data on such patients[31]. Such decision making based on previous learning requires the training model on datasets, and this kind of approach is called supervised learning. Figure 2.1 illustrates some of the application areas for AI in healthcare services and pharmacies, which are described below:

- Clinical Decision Support: AI algorithms can assess patient data such as medical history, test findings, and imaging investigations to assist clinicians in making educated decisions about diagnosis and therapy. Clinical decision support systems (CDSS) powered by AI can warn possible problems or instantly inform healthcare professionals of crucial patient information, reducing the risk of medical errors and improving patient outcomes. By giving notifications for drug interactions and individualised dose advice, CDSS can help with medication management[32]–[35].
- Medical Imaging Analysis: AI algorithms can assess patient data such as medical history, test findings, and imaging investigations to assist clinicians in making

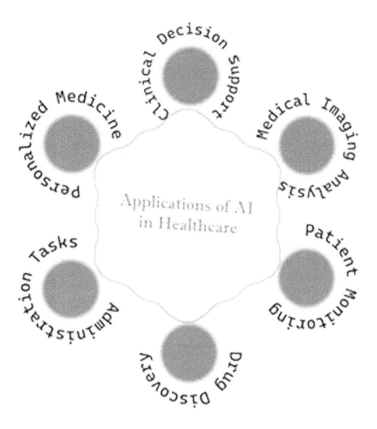

FIGURE 2.1   Applications of AI in healthcare management.

educated decisions about diagnosis and therapy. AI algorithms, for instance, can be applied to mammography images to detect early indications of breast cancer, so avoiding the need for pointless biopsies[36]–[39].

- Personalised Medicine: AI may examine patient data to create individualised treatment recommendations based on traits like genetics, way of life, and medical history. AI has the ability to spot patterns and connections that are difficult for humans to notice, resulting in more precise diagnoses and focused therapies. By avoiding unneeded treatments, personalised medicine can enhance patient outcomes and lower healthcare expenditures[40]–[42].

- Administrative Tasks: Appointment scheduling, billing, and the processing of insurance claims are just a few of the administrative chores that AI can automate. These tasks might take a while and be prone to mistakes, which would raise expenses and reduce effectiveness. Healthcare organisations can cut expenses, increase productivity, and free up personnel to concentrate on patient care by automating administrative activities[43]–[45].

- Drug Discovery: AI can analyse enormous datasets to uncover possible drug candidates and speed up the drug discovery process. AI systems can analyse genomic

TABLE 2.1   Some Medical Applications of AI

Application	Descriptions	References
Medical Imaging	Medical pictures such as X-rays, MRIs, and CT scans can be analysed by AI algorithms to assist diagnose illnesses, find anomalies, and even predict disease progression.	[36]–[39]
Electronic Health Records (EHRs)	AI has the potential to improve the accuracy and efficiency of EHRs in areas such as patient data entry, classification, and organisation. It can also help with decision support, predicting clinical outcomes, and personalised treatment planning.	[53]–[55]
Drug Discovery and Development	By analysing massive volumes of data to find possible therapeutic targets, forecast drug efficacy, and create new compounds, AI helps speed up the drug discovery process.	[46]–[48]
Remote Patient Monitoring	AI can remotely monitor patients via wearable devices and other sensors, informing healthcare personnel to any changes in the patient's condition and assisting with early diagnosis and intervention.	[49]–[52]
Clinical Decision Making	AI can assist healthcare providers in making clinical decisions, including diagnosis, treatment planning, and predicting outcomes. This can help improve patient outcomes and reduce errors.	[32]–[35]

and proteomic data to find new medication targets. AI can also forecast the efficacy and toxicity of new medication candidates, decreasing the time and money required for pre-clinical testing[46]–[48].

- Patient Monitoring: AI can remotely monitor patients' vital signs, activity levels, and medication compliance via wearable tech. Healthcare professionals can be warned about possible problems before they become serious by using AI algorithms to spot trends and anomalies in patient data. The use of remote patient monitoring can lower healthcare expenses by minimising the need for hospital stays and Emergency Room visits[49]–[52].

Artificial intelligence (AI) transforms exactly how the healthcare sector functions, by helping to enhance and improve everything to do with it, including routine tasks, data analysis and medicine development. As the healthcare field is constantly developing, it is always on the lookout for opportunities for improvement. Therefore, it should not be surprising that both healthcare providers and enterprises are adopting machine learning and AI. Some of the advantages of AI applications in healthcare are:

- Improved patient outcomes: AI can assist medical professionals in making more educated decisions regarding diagnosis and treatment, improving patient outcomes[49].
- Reduced healthcare costs: By increasing effectiveness, minimising errors, and eliminating unnecessary treatments, AI can lower healthcare expenses.

- Personalised medicine: AI may analyse patient data to create personalised treatment plans based on individual characteristics, resulting in more targeted and successful therapies.
- Faster drug discovery: AI can aid in the drug discovery process by identifying potential therapeutic candidates and anticipating their efficacy and toxicity.

While AI offers enormous potential in healthcare administration, various hurdles must be overcome, including:

- Data privacy and security: AI needs to access a lot of patient data, which raises privacy and security issues[56].
- Ethical considerations: AI algorithms may propagate bias and discrimination, raising ethical issues regarding its application in healthcare administration[57].
- Lack of standardisation: AI algorithms may propagate bias and discrimination, raising ethical issues regarding its application in healthcare administration[58].
- Implementation challenges: The use of artificial intelligence (AI) in healthcare administration can result in major benefits such as improved patient outcomes, cost savings, and increased efficiency. However, there are various difficulties related with its implementation[59].

2.3 ETHICAL CONSIDERATIONS IN ARTIFICIAL INTELLIGENCE FOR HEALTHCARE MANAGEMENT

AI has the potential to change healthcare administration, but its implementation presents fundamental ethical concerns. Data privacy and security, bias and fairness, openness and explainability, accountability and responsibility, informed consent, and regulation and governance are all important ethical considerations in AI healthcare management[60]. Healthcare organisations and AI developers must be mindful of these considerations to ensure patient safety, privacy, and equity. This includes implementing robust data privacy and security measures, monitoring and addressing biases in AI algorithms, ensuring transparency and explainability in AI systems, being accountable and responsible for outcomes, obtaining informed consent from patients, and establishing clear regulatory frameworks and governance structures. Addressing these ethical concerns in AI healthcare management is crucial for realising the potential benefits of AI while minimising potential risks to patients[61].

In addition to the ethical considerations mentioned above, there are several more significant issues that arise with the use of AI in healthcare administration. One such problem is the possibility for job displacement as AI systems automate jobs traditionally performed by humans. This raises problems regarding the responsibilities of healthcare organisations to retrain or help affected staff. Another issue is the potential for AI to aggravate current gaps in healthcare access and outcomes[62]. For example, if AI systems are trained on data that primarily reflects the experiences of certain demographic groups, they may not be effective for other groups. This underscores the importance of ensuring diversity and inclusivity in data collection and AI development.

2.4 FUTURE OF ARTIFICIAL INTELLIGENCE IN HEALTHCARE MANAGEMENT

Artificial intelligence (AI) has a bright future in healthcare administration, with numerous possible applications that might enhance patient outcomes and increase efficiency. Among the primary areas where AI is predicted to have an impact are:

- Diagnosis and treatment: Artificial intelligence systems may be trained on massive volumes of medical data to identify trends and provide trustworthy diagnoses. Based on patient data, AI can potentially be used to suggest medications and forecast outcomes[63].
- Patient monitoring: Artificial intelligence-powered technology can monitor a patient's health in real time, alerting healthcare providers to problems before they become critical.
- Drug discovery: By analysing enormous volumes of medical data, AI can find prospective medication candidates and streamline the drug development process. Medical imaging: AI can analyse medical images to identify potential issues or assist radiologists in making diagnoses.
- Operational effectiveness: By using AI, hospital operations like patient flow and personnel may be run more effectively and at a lesser cost[64].
- Personalised medicine: AI can assess patient data to develop customised treatment plans based on unique characteristics including genetics, way of life, and medical history.
- The future of AI in healthcare management will also be fraught with difficulties, including safeguarding data security and privacy, resolving biases in AI algorithms, and guaranteeing accountability and transparency in AI decision-making. Additionally, as AI in healthcare management spreads, it will be crucial to make sure that patients are at ease with and aware of how their data is being utilised[65].

Overall, the use of AI in healthcare management has a bright future because it has a wide range of possible applications that might completely change the way healthcare is provided. But in order to fully take use of AI's potential advantages, it will be crucial to solve the moral and practical issues that come with its application[66].

2.5 CASE STUDIES: SUCCESSFUL IMPLEMENTATION OF ARTIFICIAL INTELLIGENCE IN HEALTHCARE MANAGEMENT

There are numerous examples of successful artificial intelligence (AI) deployment in healthcare administration. Here are a few examples of case studies:

- IBM Watson for Oncology: An AI-powered system called IBM Watson for Oncology examines medical data to make individualised therapy suggestions for cancer patients. The system may offer therapy alternatives based on a patient's individual diagnosis and medical history after being trained on massive volumes of medical literature and actual patient data. Several hospitals around the world have implemented IBM Watson for Oncology, and studies have shown that the system can improve treatment decision-making and outcomes for cancer patients[67].

- Deep Mind Health: Deep Mind Health is a division of Google's Deep Mind that focuses on developing AI systems for healthcare management. One illustration is the Streams app, which utilises AI to help physicians detect patients with acute kidney injury (AKI). Real-time analysis of patient data by the app, which alerts doctors if it detects signs of AK, enables early intervention and better patient outcomes[68].

- The Stanford Medicine Centre for AI in Medicine & Imaging: The Stanford Medicine Centre for Artificial Intelligence in Medicine & Imaging has made it a priority to develop AI tools for managing healthcare. As an illustration, consider the ChestX-ray14 algorithm, which can analyse chest X-rays to find 14 prevalent chest disorders. The algorithm was developed after being trained on more than 100,000 photos, and it has proven to be incredibly effective in recognising diseases like pneumonia and lung cancer[69].

- Massachusetts General Hospital: In order to maximise operating room productivity, Massachusetts General Hospital has deployed a system powered by AI. For more effective scheduling and shorter patient wait times, the system uses machine learning to forecast the length of procedures and estimate the time needed for setup and cleanup[70].

These case studies demonstrate how AI has the potential to improve healthcare management in a variety of ways, including more tailored treatment recommendations and improved operational efficiency. These achievements show that AI may be a powerful tool for improving patient outcomes and modernising healthcare delivery, even in the face of challenges like concerns about data security and privacy and the requirement for transparent decision-making.

2.6 CONCLUSION

Artificial intelligence has the potential to drastically change the way healthcare is administered by improving efficiency, accuracy, and patient outcomes. From clinical decision assistance to medical image analysis, AI is increasingly being implemented into all aspects of healthcare. The AI presents numerous advantages for healthcare management, such as enhanced accuracy and precision, improved effectiveness, improved patient outcomes and others. However, there are certain additional challenges that need to be overcome in order to fully realise AI's potential in healthcare management. These challenges include ensuring the privacy and security of patient data, addressing the possibility of bias in AI algorithms, and ensuring. Overall, AI has a lot of potential to change how healthcare is managed, and by putting data privacy first, addressing bias, and working with healthcare professionals, we can make sure those AI-powered tools and systems are made to improve patient outcomes while upholding high standards of safety and ethical practise.

REFERENCES

[1] B. Zhang, J. Zhu, and H. Su, "Toward the third generation artificial intelligence," *Science China Information Sciences*, vol. 66, no. 2, pp. 121101, Jan. 2023. DOI: 10.1007/s11432-021-3449-x

[2] N. Meenigea and V. R. K. Kolla, "Exploring the current landscape of artificial intelligence in healthcare," *International Journal of Sustainable Development in Computing Science*, vol. 1, no. 1, 2023.

[3] M. Azrour, Y. Farhaoui, M. Ouanan, and A. Guezzaz, "SPIT detection in telephony over IP Using K-Means algorithm," *Procedia Computer Science*, vol. 148, pp. 542–551, 2019. DOI: 10.1016/j.procs.2019.01.027

[4] M. Mohy-eddine, A. Guezzaz, S. Benkirane, and M. Azrour, "An efficient network intrusion detection model for IoT security using K-NN classifier and feature selection," *Multimedia Tools and Applications*, 2023. DOI: 10.1007/s11042-023-14795-2

[5] J. Mabrouki, M. Azrour, D. Dhiba, and S. E. Hajjaji, "High-fidelity intelligence ventilator to help infect with COVID-19 based on artificial intelligence," in *Intelligent Data Analysis for COVID-19 Pandemic*, Springer, 2021, pp. 83–93.

[6] M. Azrour and J. Mabrouki, "Data analytics to assess the outbreak of the coronavirus epidemic: Opportunities and challenges," in *Intelligent Modeling, Prediction, and Diagnosis from Epidemiological Data*, 1st ed. Boca Raton: Chapman and Hall/CRC, 2021, pp. 47–62. DOI: 10.1201/9781003158684-3

[7] M. Azrour, J. Mabrouki, and R. Chaganti, "New efficient and secured authentication protocol for remote healthcare systems in cloud-iot," *Security and Communication Networks*, vol. 2021, pp. 1–12, May 2021. DOI: 10.1155/2021/5546334

[8] R. Chaganti, M. Azrour, R. Vinayakumar, V. Naga, A. Dua, and B. Bhushan, "A particle swarm optimization and deep learning approach for intrusion detection system in internet of medical things," *Sustainability*, vol. 14, pp. 12828, 2022.

[9] C. Hazman, S. Benkirane, A. Guezzaz, M. Azrour, and M. Abdedaime, "Building an intelligent anomaly detection model with ensemble learning for iot-based smart cities," in *Advanced Technology for Smart Environment and Energy*, Springer, 2023, pp. 287–299.

[10] G. Fattah, M. Elouardi, M. Benchrifa, F. Ghrissi, and J. Mabrouki, "Modeling of the coagulation system for treatment of real water rejects," in *Advanced Technology for Smart Environment and Energy*, Springer, 2023, pp. 161–171.

[11] R. Sriranjani, M. D. Saleem, N. Hemavathi, and A. Parvathy, "Machine learning based intrusion detection scheme to detect replay attacks in smart grid," in *2023 IEEE International Students' Conference on Electrical, Electronics and Computer Science (SCEECS)*, IEEE, 2023, pp. 1–5.

[12] M. K. Boutahir, Y. Farhaoui, and M. Azrour, "Machine learning and deep learning applications for solar radiation predictions review: Morocco as a case of study," in *Digital Economy, Business Analytics, and Big Data Analytics Applications*, Springer, 2022, pp. 55–67.

[13] M. Mohy-eddine, A. Guezzaz, S. Benkirane, and M. Azrour, "Iot-enabled smart agriculture: Security issues and applications," in *Artificial Intelligence and Smart Environment: ICAISE'2022*, Springer, 2023, pp. 566–571.

[14] J. Mabrouki *et al.*, "Smart system for monitoring and controlling of agricultural production by the IoT," in IoT and Smart Devices for Sustainable Environment, Springer, 2022, pp. 103–115.

[15] J. Mabrouki, M. Benbouzid, D. Dhiba, and S. El Hajjaji, "Internet of things for monitoring and detection of agricultural production," in Intelligent Systems in Big Data, Semantic Web and Machine Learning, Springer, 2021, pp. 271–282.

[16] A. Guezzaz, A. Asimi, A. Mourade, Z. Tbatou, and Y. Asimi, "A multilayer perceptron classifier for monitoring network traffic," in Big Data and Networks Technologies 3, Springer, 2020, pp. 262–270.

[17] A. Guezzaz, M. Azrour, S. Benkirane, M. Mohyeddine, H. Attou, and M. Douiba, "A lightweight hybrid intrusion detection framework using machine learning for edge-based iiot security," *International Arab Journal of Information Technology*, vol. 19, no. 5, 2022.

[18] A. Guezzaz, S. Benkirane, and M. Azrour, "A novel anomaly network intrusion detection system for internet of things security," in IoT and Smart Devices for Sustainable Environment, Springer, 2022, pp. 129–138.

[19] M. Douiba, S. Benkirane, A. Guezzaz, and M. Azrour, "Anomaly detection model based on gradient boosting and decision tree for IoT environments security," *Journal of Reliable Intelligent Environments*, pp. 1–12, 2022. DOI: https://doi.org/10.1007/s40 860-022-00184-3

[20] H. Attou, A. Guezzaz, S. Benkirane, M. Azrour, and Y. Farhaoui, "Cloud-based intrusion detection approach using machine learning techniques," *Big Data Mining and Analytics*, vol. 6, no. 3, pp. 311–320, 2023.

[21] M. J. Castillo and H. Taherdoost, "The impact of ai technologies on e-business," *Encyclopedia*, vol. 3, no. 1, pp. 107–121, 2023.

[22] J. N. Njoku, C. I. Nwakanma, G. C. Amaizu, and D.-S. Kim, "Prospects and challenges of metaverse application in data-driven intelligent transportation systems," *IET Intelligent Transport Systems*, vol. 17, no. 1, pp. 1–21, 2023.

[23] J. Mabrouki, G. Fattah, S. Kherraf, Y. Abrouki, M. Azrour, and S. El Hajjaji, "Artificial intelligence system for intelligent monitoring and management of water treatment plants," in Emerging Real-World Applications of Internet of Things, CRC Press, 2022, pp. 69–87.

[24] M. Azrour, J. Mabrouki, G. Fattah, A. Guezzaz, and F. Aziz, "Machine learning algorithms for efficient water quality prediction," *Modeling Earth Systems and Environment*, vol. 8, no. 2, pp. 2793–2801, 2022.

[25] J. Mabrouki, M. Azrour, and S. E. Hajjaji, "Use of internet of things for monitoring and evaluating water's quality: A comparative study," *International Journal of Cloud Computing*, vol. 10, no. 5–6, pp. 633–644, 2021.

[26] M. Mohy-Eddine, M. Azrour, J. Mabrouki, F. Amounas, A. Guezzaz, and S. Benkirane, "Embedded web server implementation for real-time water monitoring," in *Advanced Technology for Smart Environment and Energy*, J. Mabrouki, A. Mourade, A. Irshad, and S. A. Chaudhry, Eds., in Environmental Science and Engineering. Cham: Springer International Publishing, 2023, pp. 301–311. DOI: 10.1007/978-3-031-25662-2_24

[27] J. Mabrouki *et al.*, "Geographic information system for the study of water resources in chaâba el hamra, mohammedia (morocco)," in *Artificial Intelligence and Smart Environment: ICAISE'2022*, Springer, 2023, pp. 469–474.

[28] W.-C. Lin, J. S. Chen, M. F. Chiang, and M. R. Hribar, "Applications of artificial intelligence to electronic health record data in ophthalmology," *Translational Vision Science & Technology*, vol. 9, no. 2, pp. 13–13, 2020.

[29] B. Wang *et al.*, "AI-assisted CT imaging analysis for COVID-19 screening: Building and deploying a medical AI system," *Applied Soft Computing*, vol. 98, pp. 106897, Jan. 2021. DOI: 10.1016/j.asoc.2020.106897

[30] M. R. King, "The future of AI in medicine: A perspective from a Chatbot," *Annals of Biomedical Engineering*, vol. 51, no. 2, pp. 291–295, 2023.

[31] M. Chen and M. Decary, "Artificial intelligence in healthcare: An essential guide for health leaders," in *Healthcare Management Forum*, Los Angeles, CA: SAGE Publications Sage CA, 2020, pp. 10–18.

[32] S. Romero-Brufau, K. D. Wyatt, P. Boyum, M. Mickelson, M. Moore, and C. Cognetta-Rieke, "A lesson in implementation: A pre-post study of providers' experience with artificial intelligence-based clinical decision support," *International Journal of Medical Informatics*, vol. 137, pp. 104072, 2020.

[33] F. Magrabi *et al.*, "Artificial intelligence in clinical decision support: Challenges for evaluating AI and practical implications," *Yearbook of Medical Informatics*, vol. 28, no. 1, pp. 128–134, 2019.

[34] S. Montani and M. Striani, "Artificial intelligence in clinical decision support: A focused literature survey," *Yearbook of Medical Informatics*, vol. 28, no. 1, pp. 120–127, 2019.

[35] H. Haick and N. Tang, "Artificial intelligence in medical sensors for clinical decisions," *ACS Nano*, vol. 15, no. 3, pp. 3557–3567, 2021.

[36] S. Tripathi and T. H. Musiolik, "Fairness and ethics in artificial intelligence-based medical imaging," in *Research Anthology on Improving Medical Imaging Techniques for Analysis and Intervention*, IGI Global, 2023, pp. 79–90.

[37] D. Zheng, X. He, and J. Jing, "Overview of artificial intelligence in breast cancer medical imaging," *Journal of Clinical Medicine*, vol. 12, no. 2, pp. 419, 2023.

[38] N. V. Salastekar, C. Maxfield, T. N. Hanna, E. A. Krupinski, D. Heitkamp, and L. J. Grimm, "Artificial intelligence/machine learning education in radiology: Multi-institutional survey of radiology residents in the united states," *Academic Radiology*, vol. 30, pp. 1481–1487, 2023.

[39] C. Mello-Thoms and C. A. Mello, "Clinical applications of artificial intelligence in radiology," *British Journal of Radiology*, vol. 96, pp. 20221031, 2023.

[40] N. J. Schork, "Artificial intelligence and personalized medicine," *Precision Medicine in Cancer Therapy*, vol. 178, pp. 265–283, 2019.

[41] H. Sotoudeh *et al.*, "Artificial intelligence in the management of glioma: Era of personalized medicine," *Frontiers in Oncology*, vol. 9, pp. 768, 2019.

[42] A. Blasiak, J. Khong, and T. Kee, "CURATE. AI: Optimizing personalized medicine with artificial intelligence," *SLAS Technology*, vol. 25, no. 2, pp. 95–105, 2020.

[43] J. Potočnik, S. Foley, and E. Thomas, "Current and potential applications of artificial intelligence in medical imaging practice: A narrative review," *Journal of Medical Imaging and Radiation Sciences*, vol. 54, no. 2, pp. 376–385, 2023.

[44] C. Vendrami, G. Gatineau, E. Shevroja, O. Lamy, and D. Hans, "Does artificial intelligence have a role in osteoporosis management?," *Revue Medicale Suisse*, vol. 19, no. 823, pp. 752–755, 2023.

[45] Y. Y. Aung, D. C. Wong, and D. S. Ting, "The promise of artificial intelligence: A review of the opportunities and challenges of artificial intelligence in healthcare," *British Medical Bulletin*, vol. 139, no. 1, pp. 4–15, 2021.

[46] R. S. K. Vijayan, J. Kihlberg, J. B. Cross, and V. Poongavanam, "Enhancing preclinical drug discovery with artificial intelligence," *Drug Discovery Today*, vol. 27, no. 4, pp. 967–984, 2022.

[47] J. Jiménez-Luna, F. Grisoni, N. Weskamp, and G. Schneider, "Artificial intelligence in drug discovery: Recent advances and future perspectives," *Expert Opinion on Drug Discovery*, vol. 16, no. 9, pp. 949–959, 2021.

[48] J. Jiménez-Luna, F. Grisoni, and G. Schneider, "Drug discovery with explainable artificial intelligence," *Nature Machine Intelligence*, vol. 2, no. 10, pp. 573–584, 2020.

[49] T. Shaik *et al.*, "Remote patient monitoring using artificial intelligence: Current state, applications, and challenges," *Wiley Interdisciplinary Reviews: Data Mining and Knowledge Discovery*, vol. 13, no. 2, pp. e1485, 2023.

[50] A. Sujith, G. S. Sajja, V. Mahalakshmi, S. Nuhmani, and B. Prasanalakshmi, "Systematic review of smart health monitoring using deep learning and artificial intelligence," *Neuroscience Informatics*, vol. 2, no. 3, pp. 100028, 2022.

[51] P. N. Ramkumar *et al.*, "Remote patient monitoring using mobile health for total knee arthroplasty: Validation of a wearable and machine learning–based surveillance platform," *The Journal of Arthroplasty*, vol. 34, no. 10, pp. 2253–2259, 2019.

[52] J. Hathaliya, P. Sharma, S. Tanwar, and R. Gupta, "Blockchain-based remote patient monitoring in healthcare 4.0," in *2019 IEEE 9th international conference on advanced computing (IACC)*, IEEE, 2019, pp. 87–91.

[53] Y. Mintz and R. Brodie, "Introduction to artificial intelligence in medicine," *Minimally Invasive Therapy & Allied Technologies*, vol. 28, no. 2, pp. 73–81, 2019.

[54] Y. Zhou, F. Wang, J. Tang, R. Nussinov, and F. Cheng, "Artificial intelligence in COVID-19 drug repurposing," *The Lancet Digital Health*, vol. 2, no. 12, pp. e667–e676, 2020.

[55] S. M. Lauritsen *et al.*, "Explainable artificial intelligence model to predict acute critical illness from electronic health records," *Nature Communications*, vol. 11, no. 1, pp. 3852, 2020.

[56] H. Alami *et al.*, "Organizational readiness for artificial intelligence in health care: insights for decision-making and practice," *Journal of Health Organization and Management*, vol. 35, no. 1, pp. 106–114, 2021.

[57] J. S. Lim *et al.*, "Novel technical and privacy-preserving technology for artificial intelligence in ophthalmology," *Current Opinion in Ophthalmology*, vol. 33, no. 3, pp. 174–187, 2022.

[58] T. A. D'Antonoli, "Ethical considerations for artificial intelligence: An overview of the current radiology landscape," *Diagnostic and Interventional Radiology*, vol. 26, no. 5, pp. 504, 2020.

[59] Z. Allam and D. S. Jones, "On the coronavirus (COVID-19) outbreak and the smart city network: Universal data sharing standards coupled with artificial intelligence (AI) to benefit urban health monitoring and management," in *Healthcare*, MDPI, 2020, pp. 46.

[60] A. Khanijahani, S. Iezadi, S. Dudley, M. Goettler, P. Kroetsch, and J. Wise, "Organizational, professional, and patient characteristics associated with artificial intelligence adoption in healthcare: A systematic review," *Health Policy and Technology*, vol. 11, no 1, pp. 100602, 2022.

[61] S. M. Carter, W. Rogers, K. T. Win, H. Frazer, B. Richards, and N. Houssami, "The ethical, legal and social implications of using artificial intelligence systems in breast cancer care," *The Breast*, vol. 49, pp. 25–32, 2020.

[62] D. S. Char, N. H. Shah, and D. Magnus, "Implementing machine learning in health care – addressing ethical challenges," *New England Journal of Medicine*, vol. 378, no. 11, pp. 981–983, Mar. 2018. DOI: 10.1056/NEJMp1714229

[63] L. Holloway, E. Bezak, and C. Baldock, "Artificial intelligence (AI) will enable improved diagnosis and treatment outcomes," *Physical and Engineering Sciences in Medicine*, vol. 44, no. 3, pp. 603–606, 2021.

[64] A. Kerasidou, "Artificial intelligence and the ongoing need for empathy, compassion and trust in healthcare," *Bulletin of the World Health Organization*, vol. 98, no. 4, pp. 245, 2020.

[65] S. Dash, S. K. Shakyawar, M. Sharma, and S. Kaushik, "Big data in healthcare: Management, analysis and future prospects," *Journal of Big Data*, vol. 6, no. 1, pp. 1–25, 2019.

[66] G. Rong, A. Mendez, E. B. Assi, B. Zhao, and M. Sawan, "Artificial intelligence in healthcare: Review and prediction case studies," *Engineering*, vol. 6, no. 3, pp. 291–301, 2020.

[67] E. Strickland, "IBM Watson, heal thyself: How IBM overpromised and underdelivered on AI health care," *IEEE Spectrum*, vol. 56, no. 4, pp. 24–31, 2019.

[68] J. Powles and H. Hodson, "Google DeepMind and healthcare in an age of algorithms," *Health and Technology*, vol. 7, no. 4, pp. 351–367, 2017.

[69] S. Yeung, N. L. Downing, L. Fei-Fei, and A. Milstein, "Bedside computer vision-moving artificial intelligence from driver assistance to patient safety," *New England Journal of Medicine*, vol. 378, no. 14, pp. 1271–1273, 2018.

[70] J. A. Álvarez López, "Case studies of real AI applications," in *Artificial Intelligence for Business: Innovation, Tools and Practices*, Springer, 2022, pp. 141–157.

CHAPTER 3

Exploring Lung Cancer Pathologies Using Metaphoric Interventions of Deep Learning Techniques

Swapnali Patil and D. Lakshmi

3.1 INTRODUCTION

Around the world, the major public health issue is cancer. Historically, cancer has been a fatal disease. Cancer can be devasting even in this day and age of technological improvements, if not found early. Millions of lives could be saved if cancerous cells were detected as soon as possible. There are many distinct cancer types, but lung cancer is the most frequently detected worldwide. Additionally, it contributes to the highest mortality rates worldwide and is the number one cause of death (Cancer Statistics). Lung cancer early detection is useful to improve survival rates. It will also help to save lives, time, and money. Lung cancer is caused in 85% of cases by long-term tobacco use. One in five to ten percent of cases includes people who have never smoked (WHO Database, 2023).

Lung cancer is primarily divided into small cell lung carcinoma (SCLC) and non-small cell lung carcinoma (NSCLC). NSCLC accounts for 85% of lung cancer cases, while the residual 15% exists as SCLC. NSCLC is further mainly divided into adenocarcinoma (ADC), squamous cell carcinoma (SCC), and large cell carcinoma (LCC) with approximately 40%, 30% and 15% of cases respectively (Types of Lung Cancer).

Over the previous two decades, artificial intelligence (AI) and ML algorithms have acquired relevance to help people and to improve their capacity to analyze unstable data and produce stable judgments about them. Using these newest technologies, it is possible to find lung cancer in its early stages. Most research papers focused on NSCLC (Wu & Zhao 2017) invented a novel neural-network-based algorithm, entropy degradation

DOI: 10.1201/9781003430735-3

method (EDM) to detect SCLC. The CT images input are provided by the National Cancer Institute. The accuracy achieved by the algorithm was 77.6%. Improvement in the proposed method can be made with large training data and a deeper network, combined with CNN.

Lung cancer diagnosis involves three distinct methods employed by clinical experts: imaging techniques, biomarker analysis, and cytopathological or histopathological analysis.

Several imaging diagnostic methods are utilized to identify lung cancer. These techniques comprise chest radiography (CXR), computed tomography (CT), magnetic resonance imaging (MRI), and positron emission tomography (PET) scans. Traditional CXR imaging is effective in detecting lung abnormalities such as tumors or nodules. CT scans provide detailed cross-sectional lung images, enabling the identification and characterization of lung tumors. MRI scans utilize powerful magnets and radio waves to produce detailed lung images, helping in the assessment and evaluation of lung cancer and its spreading. PET scans use a radioactive tracer to highlight areas of abnormal metabolic activity, assisting in the detection and staging of lung cancer (McLoud 2002).

Biomarkers measure the progress or presence of disease. Biomarker analysis plays an important role in detecting and diagnosing cancer, including lung cancer. It involves two types of biomarkers: genetic biomarkers and blood-based biomarkers. Genetic mutations or alterations like EGFR or ALK mutations can be analyzed using techniques like polymerase chain reaction (PCR) or next-generation sequencing (NGS) to detect lung cancer and direct treatment decisions. Additionally, biomarkers present in the blood, like circulating tumor cells and circulating tumor DNA, can be analyzed to detect lung cancer and monitor treatment response (Issaq et al. 2011).

Lung cancer diagnosis can be done with cytopathological or histopathological images. Cytopathological diagnoses are safer, economical and provide quick results.

The deep convolutional neural network (DCNN) was used to classify cytological images with malignant or benign features automatically for three types of cancers. DCNN contains 3 convolutional layers, 3 pooling layers, and 2 fully connected layers. Data augmentation was performed to avoid overfitting. The original image was rotated, inverted, and filtered in the process of augmentation. In the results obtained almost 71% of the images were classified correctly. The classification accuracies for three types of cancers, ADC, SCC, and SCLC, were 89.0%, 60.0%, and 70.3%, respectively. DCNN is used for the first time by the author (Teramoto et al. 2017).

A fine-tuned VGG-16 model is used to improve the accuracy of previously used DCNN. The image patches were obtained by cropping microscopic images and then data augmentation was performed. After improvement, 81.0% accuracy is achieved by the DCNN model (Teramoto et al. 2019).

To improve DCNN's classification accuracy even more, generative adversarial network (GAN) is used to create synthesized cytological images with actual image patches. Authors introduced progressive growing of GANs (PGGAN) for high resolution of images. The DCNN model pre-trained using GAN gave a classification accuracy of

85.3%. Approximately 4.3% improvement was found as compared to the previous study (Teramoto et al. 2020).

Convolutional neural networks (CNN) and Swin transformers are used for the automatic detection of lung cancer cells. Cell nucleus segmentation using a mask R-CNN was applied to microscopic images. On the segmented images target cells were focused, ignoring background by Gaussian blurr, then a Swin transformer classification model is applied. The accuracy of the classification model using a Swin transformer is 96.16% which is nearly 2% better than a normal Resnet50 CNN model (Chen et al. 2022).

Histopathology encompasses various techniques, including tissue biopsy, immunohistochemistry, and molecular profiling. A sample of lung tissue is obtained through a biopsy procedure and checked by a pathologist to verify the presence of lung cancer cells and their features. ImmunoHistoChemistry (IHC) staining is used to detect specific proteins or biomarkers in tissue samples, which helps classify lung cancer subtypes and inform treatment decisions. techniques like fluorescent in situ hybridization (FISH) or multiplex gene panels can be employed to identify genetic alterations or gene expression patterns in lung cancer tissue. Assistance can be provided to pathologists in the detection of cancer by DL Models applied on histopathology slides (Coudray et al. 2018).

Histopathological analysis plays an important role in the detection and diagnosis of lung cancer. However, it also comes with several challenges that can affect the accuracy and reliability of the results (Lindquist et al. 2022). Some of the key challenges include tissue sample quality, tissue heterogeneity, small biopsy samples, division between benign and malignant nodules, subtyping and staging, interobserver variability, lack of specificity, integration with molecular testing, handling rare variants, frozen section analysis, and identifying emerging therapies. To address these challenges, incorporating AI and DL algorithms may assist pathologists and oncologists in making more precise and consistent diagnoses.

DL has shown great promise in enhancing histopathological analysis for the diagnosis of lung cancer. Processing histology slides and supporting pathologists in their diagnostic work are two applications that benefit from its capacity to automatically learn and extract detailed patterns from large-scale image databases (Deepapriya et al. 2023). Here are some ways DL is helpful in this context: image analysis and segmentation, feature extraction, improved accuracy and reproducibility, subtype classification, prognostic prediction, integration of image data with molecular data, integration of image data with bio-markers, speeding up diagnosis, rare variant detection, and personalized treatment.

3.2 DATASET

The basic categorization begins by utilizing a dataset that includes factors such as air pollution, alcohol drinking, and smoking as contributors to the likelihood of acquiring lung cancer. The complex dataset comprises images, gene expression data, or other biomarkers, as shown in Table 3.1.

TABLE 3.1 Lung Cancer Dataset

No	Dataset	Description	Source
1	IQ-OTHNCCD lung cancer dataset	The dataset comprises approximately 1200 CT scan images from 110 different subjects. These are divided into three separate classes: normal, benign, and malignant. Within these groups, there are 55 normal cases, 15 cases diagnosed as benign, remaining 40 as malignant cases. DICOM format was initially used for maintaining CT scan data.	Mendeley
2	Lung-PET/CT-Dx	The CT and PET/CT images of lung cancer subjects (DICOM format) are present in the dataset, along with files (XML annotation) that specify location of tumor. These images were obtained from patients suspected of having lung cancer, who subsequently underwent lung biopsies and PET/CT scans. Patients including the letter 'A' were diagnosed with ADC, 'B' with SCLC, 'E' with LCC, and 'G' with SCC along with their names/ID's.	Wiki
3	Lung cancer datasets	A diverse range of diagnostic information is accessible for identifying lung cancer, including factors like gene signatures, gene expression patterns, and biomarker indications found in gene saliva, as well as distinctions between NSLC and SCLC.	BioGPS
4	Lung histopathological images	The dataset comprises 25,000 histopathological images, divided into five distinct classes, namely: Benign tissue from the lung ADC of the lung SCC of the lung ADC of the colon Benign tissue from the colon	Kaggle
5	LIDC-IDRI	It consists of low-dose CT (LDCT) lung cancer screening.	LIDC
6	NLST	It provides LDCT screening for lung cancer.	NLST
7	TCIA	It provides various lung cancer datasets, including CT scans, PET scans, and pathology images.	The Cancer Imaging Archive
8	LIDC/IDRI	It provides CT scans of lung nodules and associated annotations provided by radiologists.	LUNA 16 Grand Challenge

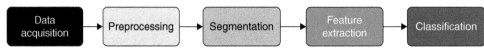

FIGURE 3.1 ML-based system for lung cancer detection.

3.3 METHODOLOGIES

Conventional ML and DL systems for the detection of lung cancer as early as possible include steps like data acquisition, preprocessing, segmentation, feature extraction, and building classification models, as shown in Figure 3.1.

3.3.1 Preprocessing

The preprocessing of data is a crucial step in the ML workflow. Various data preprocessing steps such as normalization of data, cleaning of data, resizing, and segmentation of lung

FIGURE 3.2   Data cleaning techniques.

images were performed to extract regions of interest (ROIs) (Bandyopadhyay 2019). Various post-processing techniques like Gaussian and Gabor filtering, adaptive Gaussian filtering, Wiener filtering, and CLAHE are used widely for the analysis of Image data. Preprocessing text datasets converts raw data, which contains missing values, inconsistent values, and duplicate values, to a clean data set. Data cleaning techniques are listed in Figure 3.2.

The efficient use of preprocessing techniques before the use of classification algorithms improves the classification model's precision. To achieve this improvement, 9 datasets were created using pre-processing approaches, and 6 ML classification methods were applied. According to the findings, the K-nearest neighbors (KNN) approach outperforms RF (Random Forest), NB (Naive Bayes), logistic regression, DT (Decision Tree), and SVM (Support Vector Machines) regarding precision. Using the dataset related to lung cancer, the performance of pre-processing methods was assessed. The best preprocessing methods were Z-score with 83% accuracy for normalization methods, principal component analysis with 87% accuracy for dimensionality reduction methods, and information gain with 71% accuracy for feature selection methods (Gültepe 2021).

3.3.2 Imbalanced Data

An imbalanced classification data is one with skewed class sizes. The classes that make up a high share of the data are majority classes, whereas classes that make up a smaller share of the population are minority classes. Mostly in medical decision-making, the problem of imbalanced data is observed. If training a model on an imbalanced dataset works well, then your work is done. If not, then to handle imbalanced data, downsampling or upsampling techniques are used.

Boosted SVM used for solving unbalanced data problems. This technique unites the benefits of employing several classifiers with cost-sensitive SVM for non-uniform data. In addition, for obtaining decision rules described an oracle-based method from the boosted SVM. The method's quality is then assessed by comparing its performance to that of other algorithms that work with imbalanced data. Finally, boosted SVM is utilized in medicine to estimate life expectancy following surgical operation in patients with lung cancer (Zięba et al. 2014).

To enhance the prediction performance of ML models, the authors suggested an engineering upsampling strategy (ENUS) for handling imbalanced data. The results of experiments proved that when the minority-to-majority class ratio is less than 20%, training models using ENUS enhance balanced accuracy, sensitivity, and F1 score. The research also revealed that XGBoost Tree (XGBTree) using ENUS performed the best in the validation dataset (Tran et al. 2022).

It is a tiresome and difficult task to build a medical image dataset due to various reasons like patient privacy, disease rarity, and manual efforts to collect and label data. Lack of sufficient data and imbalanced data problems are solved by using data augmentations. It artificially increases the dataset size by either data warping or oversampling. original images are transformed while preserving the labels using data-warping augmentations. This includes augmentations such as geometric and color transformations, random erasing, adversarial training, and neural style transfer. Synthetic instances are produced by oversampling augmentations and added to the training set. This includes mixing images, feature space augmentations, and generative adversarial networks (GANs) (Shorten & Khoshgoftaar 2019).

3.3.3 Segmentation

The most significant component of image processing is segmentation. A complete image is divided into many segments to make it more relevant and easier to understand. When these different portions are linked together, they will cover the full image. The numerous properties of the image may also have an impact on segmentation. It could be color or texture. An image is segmented before denoising to restore the original image. The primary goal of segmentation is to minimize the information for easier analysis. Generally, it is divided into region-based, edge-based, threshold, feature-based clustering, and model-based segmentation (Yogamangalam & Karthikeyan 2013).

The authors studied segmentation techniques for lung cancer detection like thresholding, edge detection, marker-controlled watershed segmentation, and partial differential equation (PDE) based segmentation and their comparative analysis. Marker controlled watershed segmentation provides more accurate results as compared to other segmentation techniques (Tripathi et al. 2019).

3.3.4 Feature Extraction

The process of converting raw data into digital features is very important. In feature extraction, while processing the original file information is kept intact. It gives better results than applying ML to the raw data, and features can be extracted manually or automatically to acquire beneficial and vital classification results.

Identification and justification of the features related to a particular situation are essential for manual extraction, as is the execution of a method to extract those features. solid understanding of the domain helps in making decisions about which characteristics might be useful. Through years of research, engineers and scientists have developed techniques for feature extraction from images, signals, and text.

By using special technology, features are automatically extracted from signals or images. The use of algorithms or deep networks (DN) eliminates the need for human interaction through automatic feature extraction. This approach can be quite useful when you need to quickly transition from gathering raw data to developing ML algorithms.

The first layers of DN have largely taken on the role of feature extraction with the rise of DL, albeit mostly for image data.

Image analysis technique is used for feature extraction of lung cancer and to detect tumors in lung cancer. To extract features, image processing techniques were used. The methodology followed includes the acquisition of CT lung images and then the preprocessing of CT lung images (rescaling, image enhancement, background removal, median filter). Image segmentation is done using the technique of edge detection. Feature extraction uses the gray level co-occurrence matrix (GLCM). Texture-based features were analyzed. The extracted features support the diagnosis of abnormalities in lung tissues (Alayue et al. 2022).

The author recommended a methodology which is mostly carried out in five steps.

Step 1: Images were collected from the lung cancer database. Step 2: Preprocessing was done by using the median filter technique in step two. The median filter preserves the edges i.e., sharp features are preserved. Step 3: segmentation of the target image was done using fuzzy C-means as it gives better performance than K-means Clustering. Step 4: the features were extracted using the GLCM. GLCM has high discrimination accuracy but less computational speed (autocorrelation, contrast, correlation, cluster prominence, cluster shade, dissimilarity, energy, entropy and homogeneity). Step 5: extracted features were given to the SVM classifier for the classification of lung cancer. The SVM classifier achieved an accuracy of 96.7% in detecting the type of lung cancer (Ankita et al. 2019).

The study was performed on CT images for earlier lung cancer detection. A novel method, accelerated wrapper-based binary-artificial bee colony algorithm (AWB-ABC), is used with feature extraction and an improved NB classifier. Initially, preprocessing is done using the MMSE technique for background noise elimination to acquire an improved visual image of the lung node. The AWB-ABC algorithm is used for feature selection of lung cancer nodules followed by an improved NB classifier for effectual classification (Karthiga & Rekha 2020).

Most experts agree that DNA methylation is the most important epigenetic biomarker in the mammalian genome during cancer development. Because of the large amount of noise in DNA methylation data, the prediction accuracy suffers. A solution was obtained through the utilization of a hybrid approach that relied on both attribute selection and extraction techniques. It utilizes a filter attribute selection method (F-score) and introduces an extraction model. This employs the peaks of the mean methylation density, the fast Fourier transform algorithm, and the symmetry between the methylation density of a sample as feature extraction methods. The cancer classification is done using various

ML algorithms like NB, RF, and SVM with and without hybridization. The classification accuracy improves with the proposed approach (Raweh et al. 2018).

3.3.5 Transfer Learning

The transfer learning approach is used to boost the efficiency of the model and minimize training time when adequate data for training is not available. Because the model has already been pre-trained, a good ML model can be generated with reasonably little training data using transfer learning. In transfer learning using little training data, an efficient ML model is created by a pre-trained model, as it is very difficult to obtain large training data. Figure 3.3 illustrates the generic flow with the transfer learning model.

GoogleNet – one of the most advanced CNNs in visual imagery analysis – was adjusted precisely and applied to the field of classifying malignancy in tumors. Previous studies trained simple task-specific CNNs or outdated pre-trained networks, this system increased the convergence rate and its performance metrics. To put it in another way, less training time produced better prediction results. In addition, MIPs were applied to combine multi-view information of 3D CT scans into RGB images that are similar with the fine-tuned GoogleNet. MIPs enabled the system to integrally learn features of malignant and benign lung nodules during the training, and obtain high accuracy when tested on the validation sets (Fang 2018).

In order to speed up processing, the researchers suggest a deep neural network (DNN) built onto GoogleNet that has a large dropout ratio. By utilizing the dropout layer, this network lessens overfitting during the learning process. 60% of the neurons in the suggested technique are fully linked, a lower percentage than the current GoogleNet. On the LIDC preprocess dataset, experiments were carried out utilizing the three pre-trained CNN architectures, AlexNet, GoogleNet, and ResNet50. ResNet50 produced the best accuracy of the three pre-trained architectures. Comparing the proposed network to pre-trained designs and cutting-edge techniques, it attained the best accuracy (Sajja et al. 2019).

A multi-round transfer learning and enhanced generative adversarial network algorithm is proposed with a prioritization algorithm and modified loss functions in features perspectives. It overcomes the research limitations of existing lung cancer detection

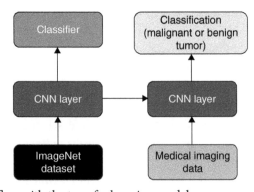

FIGURE 3.3   Generic flow with the transfer learning model.

models in multi-round transfer learning, negative transfer, and a lack of bridge between source and target domains (Chui et al. 2023).

3.3.6 Lung Cancer Classification Using ML and DL Techniques

ML techniques like the NB classifier, DT classifier, logistic regression, RF, and SVM are used for the classification of lung cancer. DL Techniques like multilayer perceptrons (MLP), artificial neural networks (ANN), CNN, back-propagation neural networks, probabilistic neural networks, SVM, and recurrent neural networks (RNN) were utilized for the identification and classification of the classifier. The use of ML and DL techniques can overcome the limitation of a shortage of pathologists with high accuracy and less time.

Lung cancer prediction from text datasets using ML focuses on providing consumers with an early warning for lung cancer, allowing them to save both money and time. From the lung cancer dataset to optimize the process of detection SVM algorithm is used efficiently (Anil Kumar et al. 2022).

Multiple methods have been used to diagnose cancer in its early stages. ML algorithms were compared in this work while detecting lung cancer nodules. To discover anomalies, authors used ML approaches such as principal component analysis, K-nearest neighbours (KNN), SVM, NB, DT, and ANN. All approaches were compared both with and without preprocessing. The testing results suggest that ANN performs best with 82.43% accuracy after image processing, and DT performs best without image processing with 93.24% accuracy (Günaydin et al. 2019).

The CNN is one of the DL models, is used frequently because of its application in the computer vision domain. The general block diagram of the DL model using CNN is shown in Figure 3.4.

The research paper provides a piece of information on the use of CNN to classify the 3 most common lung cancer types. For classification, various CNN architectures such as VGG16, InceptionV3, and InceptionResNetV2 were trained and optimized. InceptionV3 gives better classification accuracy from various architectures on the training set, so it is used on the test set. The result in the paper highlights the limitations of CNN Image classification models (Kriegsmann et al. 2020).

A novel CADe system for the early detection of lung cancer pulmonary nodules is presented. The methodology includes preprocessing of raw data, feature extraction, optimization of extracted features, and finally classification based on the optimized feature vector. For relevant feature selection, it uses the transfer learning technique. The novel CADe system accuracy has been tested, and it shows promising results in early lung cancer detection (Hekal et al. 2021).

Metabolomics research was done to identify metabolite biomarkers for the diagnosis of lung cancer. The fast correlation-based filter (FCBF) technique is used to determine the

FIGURE 3.4   General block diagram of deep learning model using CNN.

importance of a metabolic biomarker feature. Six different ML algorithms were applied to biomarker features for the early detection of lung cancer. NB showed greater accuracy out of six different ML algorithms (Xie et al. 2021).

3.3.7 Hybrid Models

hybrid models, or fusion models, are combinations of various models to get better outcomes, whereas in ensemble models, various methods are combined. Hybrid ML and DL models are usable as tools that can support clinical decision-making. The hybrid models can integrate imaging and non-imaging data and apply DL and ML models, respectively.

The research was performed to create a new feature analysis of CT images quantitatively. Then its role was examined in predicting cancer recurrence risk in stage I NSCLC patients post-surgery, along with two genomic biomarkers, namely protein expression of the excision repair cross-complementing 1 gene and a Regulatory Subunit of Ribonucleotide Reductase (RRM1). A computer-aided detection (CAD) technique was used to separate lung tumors. Tumor-related image attributes computed on chest CT images, a Naive Bayesian network-based classifier using image features and an MLP classifier utilizing genetic biomarkers underwent training to forecast cancer re-occurrence after surgery. The fusion of prediction scores provided by the two classifiers boosted prediction performance much more (Emaminejad et al. 2015).

The combination of CT images with clinical data into a multimodal data fusion model gives the best performance for the classification of lung cancer. A multimodal data fusion model created using residual learning architecture and two MLP was developed to combine CT images with patient general data and serum tumor markers (Huang et al. 2022).

A DNN model and data collection using a cloud system for dividing pulmonary sickness phases provided for classifying several stages of lung tumor advancement. As a fusion approach for PET/CT images, the suggested system makes use of a lung tumor detector and stage classifier hosted in the cloud (Cloud-LTDSC). The suggested Cloud-LTDSC used an active contour model for lung tumor segmentation, and a multilayer convolutional neural network (M-CNN) for identifying different stages of lung cancer was designed and verified using standard benchmark images (Kasinathan & Jayakumar 2022).

In this study, four DCNN models: AlexNet, GoogLeNet (Inception V3), VGG16 and ResNet50 were used to classify cytological images into ADC, SCC, and SCLC. The proper subtype classification is useful for correct treatment. For more appropriate ML classification models like NB, SVM, RF, and neural network (NN) were applied. The classification accuracies of the four DCNN models were 74.0%, 66.8%, 76.8% and 74.0%, respectively. The four ML classifiers improved overall accuracies to 75.1%, 77.5%, 78.2%, and 78.9%, respectively. The result shows improvement in classification accuracy using additional ML models with DCNN models Tsukamoto et al. (2022).

3.3.8 Evaluation Metrics

To evaluate the ML and DL models' performance, accuracy, precision, recall, F-measure, and AUC metrics were considered (Dritsas & Trigka 2022).

The performance metrics were evaluated based on the confusion matrix. It contains values which are true positive (TP), true negative (TN), false positive (FP), and false negative (FN).

$$Precision= (TP)/(TP+FP)$$

$$Recall\ (sensitivity)=(TP)/(TP+FN)$$

$$Specificity=(TN)/(TN+FP)$$

$$F\text{-}measure=(2*precision*recall) / (precision + recall)$$

$$Accuracy=(TN+TP)/(TN+TP+FN+FP)$$

Accuracy serves as an evaluation metric for classification tasks and measures the proportion of correctly predicted instances among all data instances.

Recall, also known as the true positive rate or model sensitivity, measures the model's ability to correctly identify participants who genuinely had lung cancer among all those who actually had the condition. Precision is a metric that gauges quality, whereas recall assesses quantity.

Precision is the number of participants who had lung cancer out of all the samples predicted to be positive by the model.

The F-measure is the harmonic mean of precision and recall, offering a combined score that accounts for both precision and recall in models, especially valuable when dealing with imbalanced data.

The AUC contains values between zero and one. It is a measure of classification and works to identify the ML model that performs well in differentiating lung cancer and normal cases. When the AUC value becomes 1, the models have a correct ability to differentiate between two classes. The larger values of precision, recall, specificity, F- measure, and AUC mean better performance of the model.

Table 3.2 summarizes the methodologies, datasets, performance measures, results and the future scope of research papers published in recent years 2022 and 2023.

3.4 DISCUSSION

Cancer is a condition in which a few cells from the body multiply destructively and spread to other organs. Cells typically grow and extend through cell division to produce new cells that can be used to repair old and damaged ones. This mechanism, however, gets disrupted, leading to the uncontrollable growth of aberrant cells that create tumors that can be malignant. Lung cancer is a big issue because the survival rate is low and usually it is detected at later stages. Detection of lung cancer early using ML and DL is an active area of research and development, even after a lot of technological advancement. In this paper, we reviewed ML and DL models for the early detection of lung cancer. DL algorithms have great potential to analyze large volumes of data. The fusion of DL and ML models shows greater accuracy.

TABLE 3.2 Comparison of Research Papers Published in the Year 2022, 2023

Author	Dataset	Models	Performance Measure	Future Scope	Result
Dritsas & Trigka (2022)	The Total 15 attributes used from 309 participants	Supervised ML Models (like NB, BayesNet, SGD, SVM, LR, ANN, KNN, RotF,AdaBoostM1)	RotF gives better accuracy, precision, recall and F-measure = 97.1% and an AUC of 99.3%	Use of LSTM and CNN model in research work	Binary classification
Xu et al. (2022)	Dataset from Affiliated Hospital of Hebei University and the public set. (90 patients with 619 CT images)	ISANET used channel attention and spatial attention mechanisms based on InceptionV3	For two datasets ISANET accuracy is 95.24% and 98.14% respectively, better than other CNN models	Use of unlabelled data for classification of NSLC	classification as SCC and ADC
Dwivedi et al. (2023)	The tcga_dataset is used	explainable AI (XAI)-based DL framework(, IntegratedGradients, GradientsSHAP and DeepLIFT (XaiMethods)), an autoencoder, a feed-forward neural network and a biomarker discovery module	Accuracy 95.75%	Needs to do analysis of multi omics data	A set of 52 NSCLC biomarkers discovered
Nageswaran et al. (2022)	A dataset of 83 CT images from 70 patients	Image processing and ML techniques: ANN, KNN and RF used for classification	ANN gives better classification performance	Classification to be done on more patients	Binary classification- Normal or Malignant
Pandian et al. (2022)	CT Images from Sathybama Hospital, Chennai	GoogleNet and VGG-16 CNN models used	Accuracy- 98% Specificity- 99% F1 score 98% Sensitivity- 99%	other imaging techniques used for classification	Binary classification Normal or Abnormal
Kasinathan& Jayakumar (2022)	PET/CT scans of 94 individuals	LC-Cloud system framework Multilayer CNN (M-CNN) for classification	Accuracy: 97%	To analyze more than 65 users concurrently also considering cost and security issues	Cancer stage classification

Reference	Dataset	Method	Results	Remarks	Classification
Alshmrani et al. (2023)	80000 CXR images from public datasets	VGG19 + CNN model	Loss- 0.1792 Accuracy- 96.48 Precision- 97.56 AUC- 99.82 F1- 95.62 Recall- 93.75	Two approaches- 1.Combination of CT scan images with CXR images, 2. severity level classification	Multiclass Classification for lung diseases of five different types
Bishnoi & Goel (2023)	3 types of datasets: 1. 1009 patients TCGA dataset 2. 5000 images from LC25000 3. CPTAC histopathological images	Color-based Dilated Convolutional Neural Network (CD-CNN)	Accuracy – 0.988 and AUC- 0.974	Proposed model can be trained on other modality images	Multiclass classification
Manju et al. (2023)	MRI scans of 153 people	Deep Wave Auto-Encoder (DWAE-DNN)	Precision – 98.42 Sensitivity- 100	Multiclassification to be performed	Binary classification- Malignant or Normal
Said et al. (2023)	3D CT scan data	Segmentation based on UNETR network Classification using self-supervised neural network	segmentation accuracy- 97.83%, classification accuracy- 98.77%	Proposed model is computationally intensive so it can be deployed on cloud systems or local systems	Binary classification benign or malignant
Humayun et al. (2022)	CT scan of 110 cases	CNN	accuracy VGG 16 – 98.83% VGG 19 – 98.05% Xception – 97.4 %	CT scan data integrated with other clinical data for more clarity	Normal, Benign, Malignant
Wankhade & Vigneshwari (2023)	CT scan images from LIDC/IDRI dataset called LUNA 16	Hybrid Neural Network (RNN + 3D – CNN)	selectivity- 90% sensitivity- 87% accuracy – 95%	Use of big data analysis and cascaded classifiers for more efficiency	Benign and Malignant

DL models assist pathologists and doctors to increase efficiency by reducing the time to classify tumors as malignant or benign and also providing better support for scalability. **The problems that we need to consider are:** The model's performance depends on the availability and quality of data. These automated prediction systems for lung cancer are prone to false negative results, which is a big issue in the medical field. The use of DL in medical diagnosis poses ethical concerns about patient privacy and data security. The better choice of the technique depends on several factors, the type of data collected, the number of data samples, and the time constraints. Based on many researchers' findings, the summary is that the integration of multidimensional heterogeneous data, in concurrence with the use of different methodologies for feature selection and classification, gives valuable tools for drawing inferences in lung cancer disease.

3.5 CONCLUSION

DL plays an important role in exploring lung cancer diagnosis and early prediction. Data was accepted in a variety of forms and from varied sources. Histopathological images can be used for diagnosis and classification as they contain rich information and morphological structure. From the review, we obtained data that shows CT scans are the most commonly used imaging diagnostic technique. To handle the problem of data availability, transfer learning models are used for better prediction. ML algorithms SVM and DL algorithms CNN are frequently used by researchers as they provide better accuracy. DL models are great at extracting features, and their properties can help in cancer prognosis and prediction. Data augmentation is critical for cancer diagnostic and prediction jobs to increase system performance. These methods will be critical in developing cancer diagnostic and prediction methods. However, for clinical applications, larger datasets require additional testing and validation. More study on data augmentation approaches, learning in new domains such as the frequency domain, and deploying novel architectures such as graph convolutional networks would almost certainly increase their performance. The use of ML and DL models for lung cancer is a hot research topic but these models are not yet completely implemented in practice for many reasons like security issues and tests on small datasets. By overcoming these issues, personalized AI assistants can be provided to doctors to help them with diagnosis and classification.

REFERENCES

Alayue, L. T., Goshu, B. S., & Taju, E. (2022). Feature extraction of lung cancer using image analysis techniques. *Romanian Journal of Biophysics, 32*(3), 137–154.

Alshmrani, G. M. M., Ni, Q., Jiang, R., Pervaiz, H., & Elshennawy, N. M. (2023). A deep learning architecture for multi-class lung diseases classification using chest X-ray (CXR) images. *Alexandria Engineering Journal, 64*, 923–935.

Anil Kumar, C., Harish, S., Ravi, P., Svn, M., Kumar, B. P., Mohanavel, V., & Asfaw, A. K. (2022). Lung cancer prediction from text datasets using machine learning. *BioMed Research International, 2022*, 1–10.

Ankita, R., Kumari, C. U., Mehdi, M. J., Tejashwini, N., & Pavani, T. (2019). Lung cancer image-feature extraction and classification using GLCM and SVM classifier. *International Journal of Innovative Technology Exploring. Engineering, 8*(11), 2211–2215.

Bandyopadhyay, S. K. (2019). Pre-processing and segmentation of brain image for tumor detection. *JIS University, India, 1*, 15–19.

Bishnoi, V., & Goel, N. (2023). A color-based deep-learning approach for tissue slide lung cancer classification. *Biomedical Signal Processing and Control, 86*, 105151.

Cancer statistics: 8703.00.pdf (cancer.org)

Chen, Y., Feng, J., Liu, J., Pang, B., Cao, D., & Li, C. (2022). Detection and classification of lung cancer cells using swin transformer. *Journal of Cancer Therapy, 13*(7), 464–475.

Chui, K. T., Gupta, B. B., Jhaveri, R. H., Chi, H. R., Arya, V., Almomani, A., & Nauman, A. (2023). Multiround transfer learning and modified generative adversarial network for lung cancer detection. *International Journal of Intelligent Systems, 2023*, 1–14.

Coudray, N., Ocampo, P. S., Sakellaropoulos, T., Narula, N., Snuderl, M., Fenyö, D., & Tsirigos, A. (2018). Classification and mutation prediction from non–small cell lung cancer histopathology images using deep learning. *Nature Medicine, 24*(10), 1559–1567.

Deepapriya, B. S., Kumar, P., Nandakumar, G., Gnanavel, S., Padmanaban, R., Anbarasan, A. K., & Meena, K. (2023). Performance evaluation of deep learning techniques for lung cancer prediction. *Soft Computing, 27*(13), 9191–9198.

Dritsas, E., & Trigka, M. (2022). Lung cancer risk prediction with machine learning models. *Big Data and Cognitive Computing, 6*(4), 139.

Dwivedi, K., Rajpal, A., Rajpal, S., Agarwal, M., Kumar, V., & Kumar, N. (2023). An explainable AI-driven biomarker discovery framework for Non-Small cell lung cancer classification. *Computers in Biology and Medicine, 153*, 106544.

Emaminejad, N., Qian, W., Guan, Y., Tan, M., Qiu, Y., Liu, H., & Zheng, B. (2015). Fusion of quantitative image and genomic biomarkers to improve prognosis assessment of early stage lung cancer patients. *IEEE Transactions on Biomedical Engineering, 63*(5), 1034–1043.

Fang, T. (2018, August). A novel computer-aided lung cancer detection method based on transfer learning from GoogLeNet and median intensity projections. In *2018 IEEE International Conference On Computer and Communication Engineering Technology (CCET)* (pp. 286–290). IEEE.

Gültepe, Y. (2021). Performance of lung cancer prediction methods using different classification algorithms. *Computers, Materials & Continua, 67*(2), 2015–2028.

Günaydin, Ö., Günay, M., & Şengel, Ö. (2019, April). Comparison of lung cancer detection algorithms. In *2019 Scientific Meeting on Electrical-Electronics & Biomedical Engineering and Computer Science (EBBT)* (pp. 1–4). IEEE.

Hekal, A. A., Elnakib, A., & Moustafa, H. E. D. (2021). Automated early breast cancer detection and classification system. *Signal, Image and Video Processing, 15*, 1497–1505..

Huang, H., Zheng, D., Chen, H., Wang, Y., Chen, C., Xu, L., & Li, W. (2022). Fusion of CT images and clinical variables based on deep learning for predicting invasiveness risk of stage I lung adenocarcinoma. *Medical Physics, 49*(10), 6384–6394.

Humayun, M., Sujatha, R., Almuayqil, S. N., & Jhanjhi, N. Z. (2022, June). A transfer learning approach with a convolutional neural network for the classification of lung carcinoma. *Healthcare, 10*(6), 1058. MDPI.

Issaq, H. J., Waybright, T. J., & Veenstra, T. D. (2011). Cancer biomarker discovery: Opportunities and pitfalls in analytical methods. *Electrophoresis, 32*(9), 967–975.

Karthiga, B., & Rekha, M. (2020). Feature extraction and I-NB classification of CT images for early lung cancer detection. *Materials Today: Proceedings*, *33*, 3334–3341.

Kasinathan, G., & Jayakumar, S. (2022). Cloud-based lung tumor detection and stage classification using deep learning techniques. *BioMed Research International*, *2022*, 1–17.

Kriegsmann, M., Haag, C., Weis, C. A., Steinbuss, G., Warth, A., Zgorzelski, C., & Kriegsmann, K. (2020). Deep learning for the classification of small-cell and non-small-cell lung cancer. *Cancers*, *12*(6), 1604.

Lindquist, K. E., Ciornei, C., Westbom-Fremer, S., Gudinaviciene, I., Ehinger, A., Mylona, N., & Brunnström, H. (2022). Difficulties in diagnostics of lung tumours in biopsies: An interpathologist concordance study evaluating the international diagnostic guidelines. *Journal of Clinical Pathology*, *75*(5), 302–309.

Manju, A., Kaladevi, R., Hariharan, S., Chen, S. Y., Kukreja, V., Sharma, P. K., & Wang, J. (2023). Early diagnosis of lung tumors for extending patients' life using deep neural networks. *Computers, Materials and Continua*, *76*, 993–1007.

McLoud, T. C. (2002). Imaging techniques for diagnosis and staging of lung cancer. *Clinics in Chest Medicine*, *23*(1), 123–136.

Nageswaran, S., Arunkumar, G., Bisht, A. K., Mewada, S., Kumar, J. N. V. R., Jawarneh, M., & Asenso, E. (2022). *Lung Cancer Classification And Prediction Using Machine Learning And Image Processing*. BioMed Research International, 2022.

Pandian, R., Vedanarayanan, V., Kumar, D. R., & Rajakumar, R. (2022). Detection and classification of lung cancer using CNN and Google net. *Measurement: Sensors*, *24*, 100588.

Raweh, A. A., Nassef, M., & Badr, A. (2018). A hybridized feature selection and extraction approach for enhancing cancer prediction based on DNA methylation. *IEEE Access*, *6*, 15212–15223.

Said, Y., Alsheikhy, A. A., Shawly, T., & Lahza, H. (2023). Medical images segmentation for lung cancer diagnosis based on deep learning architectures. *Diagnostics*, *13*(3), 546.

Sajja, T., Devarapalli, R., & Kalluri, H. (2019). Lung cancer detection based on ct scan images by using deep transfer learning. *Traitement du Signal*, *36*(4), 339–344.

Shorten, C., & Khoshgoftaar, T. M. (2019). A survey on image data augmentation for deep learning. *Journal of Big Data*, *6*(1), 1–48.

Teramoto, A., Tsukamoto, T., Kiriyama, Y., & Fujita, H. (2017). Automated classification of lung cancer types from cytological images using deep convolutional neural networks. *BioMed Research International*, *2017*, 1–6.

Teramoto, A., Yamada, A., Kiriyama, Y., Tsukamoto, T., Yan, K., Zhang, L.,... & Fujita, H. (2019). Automated classification of benign and malignant cells from lung cytological images using deep convolutional neural network. *Informatics in Medicine Unlocked*, *16*, 100205.

Teramoto, A., Tsukamoto, T., Yamada, A., Kiriyama, Y., Imaizumi, K., Saito, K., & Fujita, H. (2020). Deep learning approach to classification of lung cytological images: Two-step training using actual and synthesized images by progressive growing of generative adversarial networks. *PloS One*, *15*(3), e0229951.

Tran, T., Le, U., & Shi, Y. (2022). An effective up-sampling approach for breast cancer prediction with imbalanced data: A machine learning model-based comparative analysis. *Plos One*, *17*(5), e0269135.

Tripathi, P., Tyagi, S., & Nath, M. (2019). A comparative analysis of segmentation techniques for lung cancer detection. *Pattern Recognition and Image Analysis*, *29*, 167–173.

Tsukamoto, T., Teramoto, A., Yamada, A., Kiriyama, Y., Sakurai, E., Michiba, A., & Fujita, H. (2022). Comparison of fine-tuned deep convolutional neural networks for the automated classification of lung cancer cytology images with integration of additional classifiers. *Asian Pacific Journal of Cancer Prevention: APJCP*, 23(4), 1315.

Wankhade, S., & Vigneshwari, S. (2023). A novel hybrid deep learning method for early detection of lung cancer using neural networks. *Healthcare Analytics*, 3, 100195.

WHO Database (2023): www.who.int/news-room/fact-sheets/detail/lung-cancer

Wu, Q., & Zhao, W. (2017, October). Small-cell lung cancer detection using a supervised machine learning algorithm. In 2017 *International Symposium on Computer Science and Intelligent Controls (ISCSIC)* (pp. 88–91). IEEE.

Xie, Y., Meng, W. Y., Li, R. Z., Wang, Y. W., Qian, X., Chan, C., & Leung, E. L. H. (2021). Early lung cancer diagnostic biomarker discovery by machine learning methods. *Translational Oncology*, 14(1), 100907.

Xu, Z., Ren, H., Zhou, W., & Liu, Z. (2022). ISANET: Non-small cell lung cancer classification and detection based on CNN and attention mechanism. *Biomedical Signal Processing and Control*, 77, 103773.

Yogamangalam, R., & Karthikeyan, B. (2013). Segmentation techniques comparison in image processing. *International Journal of Engineering and Technology (IJET)*, 5(1), 307–313.

Zięba, M., Tomczak, J. M., Lubicz, M., & Świątek, J. (2014). Boosted SVM for extracting rules from imbalanced data in application to prediction of the post-operative life expectancy in the lung cancer patients. *Applied Soft Computing*, 14, 99–108.

CHAPTER 4

Artificial Intelligence in Smart Healthcare

Ankush Verma, Anam Mohamed Saleem,
Joyce Prabhudas Ranadive, Amit Pratap Singh Chouhan
and Vandana Singh

4.1 INTRODUCTION

Artificial intelligence (AI) has impacted a number of sectors, and its entry into the field of smart healthcare holds enormous potential for the delivery of healthcare in the future. By incorporating cutting-edge technology into the healthcare industry, smart healthcare seeks to better patient outcomes, optimize treatment programme, and expedite administrative procedures. AI-driven algorithms have the power to quickly and accurately process enormous volumes of medical data, such as patient information, medical imaging, and research articles. Artificial intelligence (AI) aids in speedier and more effective treatments, potentially saving countless lives, by identifying illnesses at an early stage and providing personalized treatment alternatives. AI has demonstrated its value in effectively managing healthcare resources[1–2]. AI systems can estimate patient demand using predictive analytics, improve hospital operations, and strategically allocate resources, ensuring that patients receive timely and effective care. This not only improves the quality of healthcare overall but also eases the strain on facilities and medical workers. Patient vital signs and health indicators may be continuously monitored in real-time thanks to the combination of wearable AI-powered gadgets and Internet of Things (IoT) technology[3]. As a result, timely interventions may be made and medical crises can be avoided by allowing remote patient monitoring[4–5]. Additionally, AI-powered virtual assistants and chatbots provide patients with round-the-clock assistance by addressing their problems, offering medical guidance, and organizing appointments, improving the availability and accessibility of healthcare services. The issues of data protection, legal compliance, and ethical concerns must be addressed as AI in the smart healthcare domain develops and matures. The success of AI-driven smart healthcare will depend heavily on maintaining patient

DOI: 10.1201/9781003430735-4

privacy and assuring ethical and transparent AI practices[6–7]. Predictive models for chronic illnesses have been developed, which is one of the important developments in AI-driven smart healthcare. AI can predict the likelihood that a patient would get a certain ailment by tracking their health data over time and fusing it with information about their lifestyle. With this proactive approach, healthcare professionals may put preventive measures and lifestyle interventions into place to reduce risks and encourage healthy living.

In the search and development of new drugs, AI is also essential. Pharmaceutical companies are using AI algorithms to examine biological data, find prospective therapeutic targets, and quicken the drug development procedure. This not only expedites the launch of new treatments but also makes it possible to provide patients with personalized healthcare based on their genetic profiles. Since AI technology has been incorporated, telemedicine and virtual healthcare have significantly increased. Before patients contact with real healthcare providers, AI-driven telemedicine platforms may carry out early evaluations, help with patient triage, and offer preliminary diagnosis[8–10]. This strategy eases the burden on healthcare systems and increases access to healthcare, particularly in isolated or disadvantaged regions. AI can improve patient involvement and adherence to treatment strategies. Patients may learn more about their diseases, be reminded to take their prescriptions and be encouraged to adopt healthy lifestyle choices with the help of personalized AI-powered applications and digital health coaches. This involvement strengthens the patient-provider bond and equips people to take charge of their own health[11–12] Additionally, AI may be used to develop personalized treatment regimens, find new therapeutic targets, and improve clinical trial designs, opening the way for more efficient and individualized medical procedures. However, the use of AI in smart healthcare also poses ethical, legal, and societal issues. To create an ethical and reliable AI ecosystem, it is crucial to pay attention to issues like protecting data privacy, preventing algorithmic bias, and ensuring openness in AI decision-making[13–15].

Along with the improvements, AI in smart healthcare is promoting the expansion of precision medicine. Precision medicine makes medical decisions based on each patient's unique traits, taking into account their environment, lifestyle, and genetics. Healthcare providers can deliver personalized treatment plans that are more effective and targeted by utilizing AI's capacity to analyse vast amounts of genomic data and integrate it with clinical and lifestyle data. This increases the likelihood of successful outcomes and reduces the likelihood of medication side effects. Medical imaging and diagnostics are being transformed by AI as well. X-rays, CT scans, and MRI scans may all be accurately analyzed by AI using deep learning algorithms. With the use of these algorithms, doctors may discover illnesses in their early stages and make quicker, more accurate diagnoses because they can spot minute features that would not be evident to the human eye. This allows for quicker treatments, which improves patient outcomes while also saving time[16–17].

The method that medical research uses is changing as a result of AI. Researchers may more quickly find possible treatments, better understand disease causes, and make choices based on the best available evidence thanks to AI's ability to collect and analyze enormous volumes of clinical trial and scientific journal data. Additionally increasing popularity is the use of AI in operating rooms. Artificial intelligence-powered robotic surgery allows for more accuracy, dexterity, and stability during difficult procedures. The ability to operate with more accuracy lowers the possibility of problems and speeds up patient recovery. Healthcare professionals may anticipate patient requirements, avoid readmissions to the hospital, and allocate resources more efficiently with the use of AI-based predictive analytics. AI can identify high-risk patients who may need more attention by examining patient data and historical trends. This enables healthcare workers to take early action and avert future health disasters[18–21].

Diagnostics, therapy, patient involvement, and healthcare delivery are all seeing dramatic changes as a result of the use of AI in smart healthcare, which is transforming the medical environment. The healthcare sector can fully utilize AI's potential to enhance patient outcomes, lower healthcare costs, and build a more sustainable and patient-centric healthcare system by adopting AI ethically and cooperatively.

4.2 EMERGENCE OF SMART HEALTHCARE: A REVOLUTION POWERED BY AI

Smart healthcare represents a disruptive shift propelled by the power of artificial intelligence (AI). This model change makes use of AI's capacity to quickly and effectively analyze enormous volumes of medical data, resulting in improved diagnosis, individualized treatment regimens, and proactive disease prevention[22–24]. The field of smart healthcare is ready to provide more effective, affordable, and patient-centered solutions, from predictive analytics that foresee disease outbreaks to wearable technology that continuously records vital signs. As AI develops further, its incorporation into healthcare systems holds the prospect of revolutionizing patient care by making it more individualized, accurate, and accessible. A technology revolution headed by smart healthcare is being driven by artificial intelligence (AI), which has unmatched potential. By utilizing AI's ability to quickly analyze and interpret massive amounts of medical data, this revolutionary change is completely changing the face of healthcare[25–27]. Advanced algorithms and machine learning enable AI-driven smart healthcare systems to give quick and precise diagnoses, spot trends that human practitioners would miss, and ease the creation of individualized treatment routes. With wearable technology and remote monitoring tools, patients may take an active role in their healthcare management outside of the clinic. The blending of technology and healthcare holds the possibility of improving preventive measures, streamlining the workflows of medical personnel, and eventually improving patient outcomes on a never-before-seen scale. Smart healthcare is a paradigm change in the medical industry, supported by artificial intelligence's (AI) revolutionary potential. This revolution involves reinventing healthcare procedures as well as technological integration[28–31]. Early illness diagnosis, accurate diagnoses, and the creation of individualized treatment plans are all made possible by AI's amazing capacity for quick data processing. The convergence of AI and healthcare also applies to telemedicine, where chatbots with AI-powered virtual health consultations offer accessible and quick medical advice. Additionally, predictive analytics assist health organizations in planning ahead for epidemics, effectively allocating resources, and developing preventive approaches. Patients may now actively monitor their health parameters thanks to the advent of wearable technology, which is promoting a culture of preventive care. While there are still issues, such as data privacy and ethical concerns, the age of smart healthcare powered by AI offers unmatched prospects to transform medical procedures, better patient experiences, and eventually improve global health outcomes[32–33].

4.3 LEVERAGING AI FOR EFFICIENT MEDICAL IMAGING AND DIAGNOSIS

A significant development in the field of healthcare is the use of AI for effective medical imaging and diagnostics. Medical imaging procedures are improved with unmatched precision and speed by utilizing artificial intelligence. In imaging like X-rays, MRIs, and CT scans, AI systems can quickly analyze minute details, spotting tiny irregularities that a human eye would miss[34–36]. This not only speeds up the diagnosis procedure but also lowers the chance of human mistake. Medical imaging systems powered by AI may learn from enormous datasets, gradually increasing their diagnosis precision. By the use of enhanced insights, this technology gives radiologists and doctors the capacity to make better judgments and present detailed treatment recommendations. The potential for AI to transform medical imaging and diagnosis is limitless as it develops, offering quicker and more accurate diagnoses, lower healthcare costs, and ultimately better patient outcomes. A significant development in healthcare is the application of AI to medical imaging and diagnostics[37–39]. An unrivalled level of accuracy and efficiency is made possible for medical practitioners by this combination. For example, MRI, CT, and PET scan pictures may be quickly and effectively analyzed by AI algorithms, allowing for the early identification of tiny anomalies suggestive of a variety of illnesses. Deep learning enables AI systems to continually improve their comprehension of patterns and variances within medical imagery, leading to ever-more accurate diagnoses. This game-changing technology not only accelerates the diagnosis, allowing for a speedier start to treatment, but it also frees up radiologists and doctors from mundane duties so they can concentrate on more difficult and urgent situations. By offering in-depth insights and making diagnosis suggestions, AI acts as a beneficial second opinion to complement their knowledge[41–41].

AI's computational skills may be used to analyze and interpret medical pictures quickly and accurately. AI algorithms are very good at seeing complex patterns in photos, which helps in the early diagnosis of abnormalities like tumors or fractures that can be difficult to spot using conventional techniques. This reduces the likelihood of oversight while also quickening the diagnostic process. AI-driven systems continually learn from enormous datasets, improving the accuracy of their diagnoses over time[3,42–43]. Medical practitioners may deliver individualized treatment plans, properly distribute resources, and improve their workflow with the help of AI. As AI technology develops, it has limitless potential to reinvent medical imaging and diagnostics, offering better patient care, efficient resource use, and a new strategy for addressing healthcare concerns.

4.4 AI-DRIVEN PREDICTIVE ANALYTICS FOR PREVENTIVE HEALTHCARE

AI-driven predictive analytics is revolutionizing the landscape of preventive healthcare by harnessing the power of advanced algorithms and big data to anticipate and mitigate potential health risks before they escalate into serious conditions[44]. This cutting-edge approach utilizes the union of artificial intelligence, machine learning, and predictive modeling to identify patterns, detect anomalies, and forecast health trends within populations and individuals. By analyzing an extensive range of medical records, lifestyle data, genetic information, and environmental factors, AI-driven predictive analytics holds the promise of transforming healthcare from a reactive system to a proactive one, focusing on early intervention and personalized strategies to keep individuals healthy. One of the most significant advantages of AI-driven predictive analytics in preventive healthcare is its ability to leverage historical patient data to forecast future health outcomes. Traditional healthcare systems often rely on retrospective analysis of medical histories, leading to delays in detecting potential health risks. However, AI algorithms can examine through vast amounts of data to identify subtle correlations that might go unnoticed by human clinicians. For instance, an individual's electronic health records, combined with data from wearable and lifestyle habits, can be used to predict the likelihood of developing chronic diseases such as diabetes, cardiovascular issues, or even mental health disorders. By recognizing patterns that indicate early stages of these conditions, healthcare providers can tailor interventions and treatment plans to prevent the escalation of illnesses[45–47].

AI-driven predictive analytics fosters personalized healthcare strategies, acknowledging that each individual is unique, and their health journeys are distinct. By analyzing genetic information, family history, and lifestyle choices, AI algorithms can develop personalized risk profiles for patients. This enables healthcare professionals to offer targeted recommendations that encompass dietary adjustments, exercise routines, and screenings tailored to a person's specific susceptibilities. For instance, if the algorithm identifies a genetic predisposition to a certain type of cancer, it can prompt regular screenings and preemptive measures, thereby significantly improving the chances of early detection and successful treatment. AI-powered predictive analytics aids in optimizing resource allocation within healthcare systems. By identifying high-risk individuals, hospitals and healthcare providers can allocate their resources more efficiently, focusing on those who are most likely to require medical attention. This not only enhances patient care but also alleviates strain on healthcare facilities, enabling them to better prepare for potential surges in demand. As a result, this approach contributes to a more sustainable and cost-effective healthcare system.

The implementation of AI-driven predictive analytics in preventive healthcare does raise ethical and privacy concerns. The access and utilization of vast amounts of personal health data require stringent security measures to safeguard patient confidentiality. Striking the right balance between data accessibility and privacy is crucial to ensure that the potential benefits of this technology are not overshadowed by breaches of trust or misuse of sensitive information. Careful attention must be paid to ethical considerations to uphold patient privacy and trust. As this field continues to evolve, the collaboration between technology experts, healthcare professionals, and policymakers will be pivotal in harnessing the full potential of AI-driven predictive analytics for the betterment of global healthcare.

4.5 PERSONALIZED TREATMENT PLANS THROUGH AI-DRIVEN INSIGHTS

In the realm of healthcare, the advent of artificial intelligence (AI) has piloted in a new era of precision and personalization, revolutionizing the way medical treatments are conceptualized and administered. AI-driven insights are now empowering healthcare professionals to craft personalized treatment plans that are finely tailored to each individual's distinct characteristics and needs. This paradigm shift holds immense promise, not only in enhancing the efficacy of treatments but also in reducing adverse effects and improving overall patient outcomes. The ability of AI algorithms to analyze vast and intricate datasets with remarkable speed and accuracy. By assimilating a patient's medical history, genetic information, lifestyle choices, and even real-time physiological data, AI systems can uncover subtle patterns and correlations that would have remained elusive through traditional methods[48–50]. This treasure trove of insights enables clinicians to make informed decisions that align with the unique biology of each patient. AI can identify genetic predispositions that may influence the way an individual metabolizes certain medications, allowing doctors to prescribe drugs that are more likely to be effective and less likely to cause adverse reactions.

Predictive analytics models can anticipate potential health issues based on a person's profile and behavior, enabling early interventions that mitigate the progression of diseases. AI algorithm could detect subtle markers that indicate a heightened risk of cardiovascular problems in a middle-aged individual with a family history of heart disease. Healthcare providers can design a personalized plan that includes lifestyle modifications and monitoring strategies to prevent or delay the onset of serious conditions. It's important to note that while AI-driven personalized treatment plans hold immense promise, they are not intended to replace the human touch in medicine. Rather, they serve as a powerful tool that complements the expertise of healthcare professionals. The clinician's role evolves from making decisions based on limited information to collaborating with AI systems that provide a comprehensive and nuanced understanding of the patient's health[51–52]. Technological advancements are challenges that must be addressed. One of the primary concerns is the ethical use of patient data. The success of AI-driven personalized treatment plans relies on the availability of extensive and diverse datasets. Safeguarding patient privacy and ensuring data security are paramount to building and maintaining public trust in these systems. Striking the right balance between data utilization and patient confidentiality is a complex task that requires stringent regulations and transparent practices.

Medical education must adapt to include training in AI concepts and applications to ensure that clinicians can effectively interpret and utilize the insights provided by these systems[53–54]. Bridging this knowledge gap is essential to harnessing the full potential of AI-driven personalized treatment plans and guaranteeing their seamless integration into clinical practice.

The era of personalized treatment plans powered by AI-driven insights is reshaping the landscape of healthcare. The convergence of advanced data analytics, machine learning, and medical expertise heralds a future where treatments are tailored to the individual, maximizing effectiveness and minimizing risks[55]. As the field of AI in healthcare continues to evolve, it is imperative that stakeholders collaborate to address challenges, ensuring that these transformative technologies are deployed ethically, effectively, and for the betterment of global health[56–58].

4.6 ENHANCING PATIENT CARE WITH AI-ENABLED REMOTE MONITORING

Enhancing patient care with AI-enabled remote monitoring marks a striking paradigm change in the healthcare industry, ushering in a new era of individualized, proactive, and patient-centric medical treatment. This novel method makes use of artificial intelligence to close geographic gaps, make the best use of healthcare resources, and offer ongoing, real-time insights into a patient's health. Healthcare providers can remotely gather a wealth of physiological data using wearable tech, intelligent sensors, and cutting-edge algorithms, including vital signs like heart rate, blood pressure, and oxygen saturation as well as more complicated metrics like sleep patterns, activity levels, and even ECG readings. The potential of AI-enabled remote monitoring to support early identification and intervention, which transforms the way chronic illnesses are managed, is its main benefit[59]. By continuously monitoring and analyzing data, anomalies and patterns that may otherwise go undetected can be quickly found, allowing medical practitioners to take action before small problems turn into serious health emergencies. Lowering hospital admissions and ER visits not only improves patient outcomes but also lessens the demand on medical institutions. AI-enabled remote monitoring encourages a sense of empowerment and accountability by giving people access to their health data in real-time via user-friendly applications or web platforms. Patients can get a better understanding of their physical well-being and trends and make more educated decisions about their lifestyle, medication adherence, and overall treatment. AI and remote monitoring together have the power to completely transform medical care. This strategy represents a patient-centered healthcare paradigm that has the potential to improve outcomes, increase quality of life, and transform the healthcare landscape by providing a holistic perspective of a patient's health, enabling early treatments, and encouraging patient participation[60].

4.7 ROBOTIC ASSISTANTS IN HEALTHCARE: AI'S IMPACT ON SURGICAL PROCEDURES

Artificial intelligence-powered robotic assistants are being integrated into healthcare, which has transformed surgery and pushed the limits of accuracy, effectiveness, and patient outcomes. As extensions of experienced surgeons, these cutting-edge AI-driven robotic devices provide improved dexterity, precision, and control during difficult surgeries. These robotic helpers, which are outfitted with complex sensors, cameras, and AI algorithms, offer real-time feedback, 3D visualization, and predictive insights, enabling surgeons to maneuver through complex anatomical systems with unmatched accuracy. Robotic assistants powered by AI have significantly transformed minimally invasive operations, which involve smaller incisions, less discomfort, and faster patient recoveries. These surgical robots can read imaging data with the help of AI algorithms, build precise 3D representations of the patient's anatomy, and even adjust in real-time to changes that occur during surgery. In addition to streamlining the surgical procedure, this adaptive capability also reduces the hazards brought on by human mistake[61]. As these systems can analyze enormous quantities of previous surgical data and simulate numerous scenarios to help in decision-making, the incorporation of AI into surgical operations shortens the learning curve for surgeons. Through virtual practice and instruction, surgeons may hone their abilities and promote expertise and continual progress. Surgical treatment is becoming safer, more standardized, and more widely available thanks to the symbiotic relationship between human surgeons and AI-driven robotic helpers. However, the development of AI-driven robotic helpers also brings up moral, legal, and financial issues. Aspects that must be carefully taken care of include ensuring patient safety, guarding against technological problems, and managing liability issues. Furthermore, there are issues with price, integration, and training due to the accessibility of such cutting-edge technology in a variety of healthcare settings, including those with limited resources. A turning point in medical history has been reached with the integration of AI and robots in healthcare, particularly in surgical operations. Robotic assistants powered by AI are redefining the limits of what can be accomplished during surgical operations thanks to their accuracy, flexibility, and promise for better patient outcomes[62]. The joint synergy between human knowledge and AI-driven robots promises a future in which operations are not simply procedures, but finely tuned arts that optimize recovery and well-being as technology continues to advance and healthcare systems adapt.

4.8 OVERCOMING CHALLENGES IN IMPLEMENTING AI IN HEALTHCARE SETTINGS

Artificial intelligence (AI) use in healthcare settings has unquestionably become a disruptive strategy with the ability to improve patient care, diagnosis, treatment, and administrative procedures. One of the biggest obstacles is the sensitive and complicated nature of healthcare data, which includes patient records, imaging data, and genetic data[63]. The smooth integration of AI applications into current healthcare procedures might be hampered by technical difficulties, such as problems with interoperability across various electronic health record systems. It is crucial to create AI models that can be explained and offer clear insights into decision-making procedures. AI model training and validation may be hampered by the lack of high-quality, annotated healthcare datasets. For patient safety and efficacy, it is crucial to establish strong validation frameworks that take into account the dynamic nature of AI. Also important is bridging the knowledge gap between clinical practitioners and AI developers. Clinicians frequently lack the technical knowledge necessary to properly understand AI systems, making good multidisciplinary communication and training initiatives necessary. Another difficulty is overcoming financial limitations[64]. The long-term advantages of implementing AI in healthcare seem encouraging, but there is a significant upfront cost for infrastructure, software, and staff training. Healthcare organizations need to develop long-term financial plans that take into account possible returns on investment. The path to integrating AI into healthcare environments is paved with tremendous obstacles that cut across the technological, governmental, cultural, and financial spectrums. Collaboration between healthcare practitioners, researchers, politicians, and technological specialists is required to overcome these obstacles. The healthcare sector can fully utilize AI to improve patient outcomes, expedite processes, and transform the future of medicine by solving challenges of data protection, transparency, validation, and multidisciplinary collaboration[65].

4.9 ETHICAL CONSIDERATIONS AND PRIVACY CONCERNS IN AI-DRIVEN HEALTHCARE

In the field of AI-driven healthcare, where novel technologies have the potential to revolutionize patient care and diagnosis, ethical considerations and privacy issues are of utmost relevance. Although these developments have great potential, they also present difficult moral questions and privacy issues that call for close examination. The ethical and open use of patient data is one of the main issues. To train and improve their algorithms, AI systems frequently use huge datasets that contain sensitive medical data. To stop unauthorized access, data breaches, and potential exploitation of personal health records, patient privacy protection becomes essential[64].

The responsibility and transparency of AI algorithms provide further ethical consideration. Understanding the logic behind some AI models' conclusions can be difficult because of their 'black-box' nature, which is especially problematic in situations involving patient safety. Transparency is key to building confidence in AI-driven systems since patients and healthcare professionals have a right to know the rationale behind a given diagnosis or advised course of treatment. The potential applications of AI in healthcare are vast, but they are also complicated by serious privacy and ethical issues. Healthcare practitioners, technologists, ethicists, and politicians must work together across disciplines to address difficulties such as balancing innovation with patient privacy, openness, bias reduction, and keeping the human aspect in healthcare delivery. Utilizing AI's full potential while preserving the fundamental principles of medical ethics and patient welfare will need a deliberate, inclusive, and human-centered approach[66].

4.10 THE FUTURE OF AI IN SMART HEALTHCARE: TRENDS AND POTENTIAL INNOVATIONS

The future of artificial intelligence in smart healthcare has enormous promise, powered by the confluence of cutting-edge technology and an increasing emphasis on personalized, efficient, and patient-centric healthcare solutions. As time goes on, numerous important themes will define the future of AI in healthcare. One of the most important advances is the use of AI-driven predictive analytics, which enables healthcare professionals to forecast disease outbreaks, patient deterioration, and treatment responses with remarkable precision. This not only improves patient care but also allows healthcare institutions to better allocate resources. The improvement of medical specialists using AI-driven decision support systems is another important development. In order to offer doctors suggestions that are supported by evidence, these systems sift through enormous volumes of patient data, scientific literature, and clinical guidelines[67]. As a result, physicians are better equipped to make judgments that are fast and accurate. The potential for artificial intelligence to revolutionize medication research is astounding. AI algorithms can mimic molecular interactions, forecast drug interactions, and speed up the identification of possible drug candidates, which greatly cuts down on the time and expense needed to introduce new medications to the market[68]. AI's capacity to analyze a person's genetic composition and match it with customized treatment choices, minimizing side effects and maximizing therapeutic benefits, makes personalized medicine increasingly attainable. AI's potential to alter the healthcare business in the future, from diagnosis and treatment to patient engagement and operational effectiveness, is enormous[69].

4.11 CONCLUSION

Finally, the integration of artificial intelligence (AI) and healthcare offers a strikingly promising horizon for the reform of medical practices and patient outcomes. The use of AI technology in different aspects of healthcare, such as diagnosis, treatment, drug development, and patient management, has demonstrated enormous potential to revolutionize how medical personnel function and patients get care. AI-based diagnostic systems, powered by modern machine learning algorithms, have proven exceptional accuracy in diagnosing a variety of illnesses from medical imaging, allowing for early intervention and greatly improving treatment success rates. AI-powered healthcare systems are also promoting predictive analytics, which may forecast disease outbreaks and health trends, providing public health organizations with timely information for strategic responses. Drug discovery, which has traditionally been a time-consuming and expensive process, is benefiting from AI's capacity to rapidly analyze large datasets and forecast possible drug candidates, dramatically lowering the time and money necessary for research and development. AI-powered virtual health assistants and chatbots improve patient engagement and adherence by delivering personalized information and assistance, significantly increasing the reach of healthcare services. To prevent AI technologies from unintentionally worsening current healthcare inequities or undermining patient trust, ethical issues relating to data privacy, algorithm bias, and openness in decision-making processes need to be carefully considered. To keep up with the rapid breakthroughs in AI, regulatory frameworks must be flexible and adaptable in order to guarantee patient safety and the effectiveness of medical interventions. The bright future of AI-supported healthcare transformation has the potential to change the medical industry by bringing more precise diagnoses, individualized therapies, proactive disease management, and accelerated drug development procedures. We are on the precipice of a new age when technology and medicine intersect to deliver more accessible, effective, and patient-centered care. This era will be ushered in by navigating the difficulties and using the strengths of AI in healthcare.

REFERENCES

1. Tariq A, Gill AY, Hussain HK. Evaluating the potential of artificial intelligence in orthopedic surgery for value-based healthcare. *International Journal of Multidisciplinary Sciences and Arts*. 2023 Jun 9;2(1):27–35.
2. Patil S, Shankar H. Transforming healthcare: Harnessing the power of AI in the modern era. *International Journal of Multidisciplinary Sciences and Arts*. 2023 Jul 10;2(1):60–70.
3. Rejeb A, Rejeb K, Treiblmaier H, Appolloni A, Alghamdi S, Alhasawi Y, Iranmanesh M. The Internet of Things (IoT) in healthcare: Taking stock and moving forward. *Internet of Things*. 2023 Feb 14:100721.
4. Tagde P, Tagde S, Bhattacharya T, Tagde P, Chopra H, Akter R, Kaushik D, Rahman MH. Blockchain and artificial intelligence technology in e-Health. *Environmental Science and Pollution Research*. 2021 Oct 28;52:810–31.
5. Harry A. The future of medicine: Harnessing the power of AI for revolutionizing healthcare. *International Journal of Multidisciplinary Sciences and Arts*. 2023 Jun 9;2(1):36–47.
6. Gerke S, Minssen T, Cohen G. Ethical and legal challenges of artificial intelligence-driven healthcare. In *Artificial Intelligence in Healthcare*. 2020 Jan 1 (pp. 295–336). Academic Press.
7. Chauhan C, Gullapalli RR. Ethics of AI in pathology: Current paradigms and emerging issues. *The American Journal of Pathology*. 2021 Oct 1;191(10):1673–83.
8. Jadczyk T, Wojakowski W, Tendera M, Henry TD, Egnaczyk G, Shreenivas S. Artificial intelligence can improve patient management at the time of a pandemic: The role of voice technology. *Journal of Medical Internet Research*. 2021 May 25;23(5):e22959.
9. Aggarwal N, Ahmed M, Basu S, Curtin JJ, Evans BJ, Matheny ME, Nundy S, Sendak MP, Shachar C, Shah RU, Thadaney-Israni S. Advancing artificial intelligence in health settings outside the hospital and clinic. *NAM Perspectives*. 2020;2020:1–26.
10. El-Miedany Y. Telehealth and telemedicine: How the digital era is changing standard health care. *Smart Homecare Technology and Telehealth*. 2017 Jun 20:43–51.
11. Panesar A. *Machine Learning and AI for Healthcare*. Coventry, UK: Apress, 2019.
12. Panesar A, Panesar H. Artificial intelligence and machine learning in global healthcare. In *Handbook of Global Health*. 2021 May 12 (pp. 1775–1813). Cham: Springer International Publishing.
13. Cobianchi L, Verde JM, Loftus TJ, Piccolo D, Dal Mas F, Mascagni P, Vazquez AG, Ansaloni L, Marseglia GR, Massaro M, Gallix B. Artificial intelligence and surgery: Ethical dilemmas and open issues. *Journal of the American College of Surgeons*. 2022 Aug 1;235(2):268–75.
14. Albahri AS, Duhaim AM, Fadhel MA, Alnoor A, Baqer NS, Alzubaidi L, Albahri OS, Alamoodi AH, Bai J, Salhi A, Santamaría J. A systematic review of trustworthy and explainable artificial intelligence in healthcare: Assessment of quality, bias risk, and data fusion. *Information Fusion*. 2023 Aug;96:156–191.
15. Dara R, Hazrati Fard SM, Kaur J. Recommendations for ethical and responsible use of artificial intelligence in digital agriculture. *Frontiers in Artificial Intelligence*. 2022 Jul 29;5:884192.

16. Aggarwal R, Sounderajah V, Martin G, Ting DS, Karthikesalingam A, King D, Ashrafian H, Darzi A. Diagnostic accuracy of deep learning in medical imaging: A systematic review and meta-analysis. *NPJ Digital Medicine*. 2021 Apr 7;4(1):65.

17. Tadiboina SN. The use of AI in advanced medical imaging. *Journal of Positive School Psychology*. 2022 Nov 25;6(11):1939–46.

18. Dawoodbhoy FM, Delaney J, Cecula P, Yu J, Peacock I, Tan J, Cox B. AI in patient flow: Applications of artificial intelligence to improve patient flow in NHS acute mental health inpatient units. *Heliyon*. 2021 May 1;7(5):e06993.

19. Dash S, Shakyawar SK, Sharma M, Kaushik S. Big data in healthcare: Management, analysis and future prospects. *Journal of Big Data*. 2019 Dec;6(1):1–25.

20. Lee EE, Torous J, De Choudhury M, Depp CA, Graham SA, Kim HC, Paulus MP, Krystal JH, Jeste DV. Artificial intelligence for mental health care: Clinical applications, barriers, facilitators, and artificial wisdom. *Biological Psychiatry: Cognitive Neuroscience and Neuroimaging*. 2021 Sep 1;6(9):856–64.

21. Chan CY, Petrikat D. Strategic applications of artificial intelligence in healthcare and medicine. *Journal of Medical and Health Studies*. 2023 Jun 8;4(3):58–68.

22. M. Bublitz F, Oetomo A, S. Sahu K, Kuang A, X. Fadrique L, E. Velmovitsky P, M. Nobrega R, P. Morita P. Disruptive technologies for environment and health research: An overview of artificial intelligence, blockchain, and internet of things. *International Journal of Environmental Research and Public Health*. 2019 Oct;16(20):3847.

23. Concepcion RS, Bedruz RA, Culaba AB, Dadios EP, Pascua AR. The technology adoption and governance of artificial intelligence in the Philippines. In *2019 IEEE 11th International Conference on Humanoid, Nanotechnology, Information Technology, Communication and Control, Environment, and Management (HNICEM)*. 2019 Nov 29 (pp. 1–10). IEEE.

24. Bajwa J, Munir U, Nori A, Williams B. Artificial intelligence in healthcare: transforming the practice of medicine. *Future Healthcare Journal*. 2021 Jul;8(2):e188.

25. Kalhotra SK, Pandey SK, Verma P, Dahiya V. *Smart Technologies for Sustainable Development*. 2023 Aug 2, Booksclinic Publishing.

26. Marcus G, Davis E. Rebooting AI: Building artificial intelligence we can trust. 2019 Sep 10, Vintage.

27. McQuillan D. *Resisting AI: An anti-fascist approach to artificial intelligence*. Policy Press. 2022.

28. Ismail S. Exponential organizations: Why new organizations are ten times better, faster, and cheaper than yours (and what to do about it). *Diversion Books*. 2014 Oct 14.

29. Prowell S, Manz D, Culhane C, Ghafoor S, Kalke M, Keahey K, Matarazzo C, Oehmen C, Peisert S, Pinar A. *Position Papers for the ASCR Workshop on Cybersecurity and Privacy for Scientific Computing Ecosystems*. 2021 Nov 1, US Department of Energy (USDOE), Washington DC (United States). Office of Science.

30. Cheng L, Chan WK, Peng Y, Qin H. Towards data-driven tele-medicine intelligence: Community-based mental healthcare paradigm shift for smart aging amid COVID-19 pandemic. *Health Information Science and Systems*. 2023 Mar 14;11(1):14.

31. Alabdulatif A, Khalil I, Yi X, Guizani M. Secure edge of things for smart healthcare surveillance framework. *IEEE Access*. 2019 Feb 27;7:31010–21.

32. Althobaiti K. Surveillance in next-generation personalized healthcare: Science and ethics of data analytics in healthcare. *The New Bioethics*. 2021 Oct 2;27(4):295–319.

33. Joshi S, Bisht B, Kumar V, Singh N, Jameel Pasha SB, Singh N, Kumar S. Artificial intelligence assisted food science and nutrition perspective for smart nutrition research and healthcare. *Systems Microbiology and Biomanufacturing.* 2023 Aug 9:1–6.

34. Tadiboina SN. The use of AI in advanced medical imaging. *Journal of Positive School Psychology.* 2022 Nov 25;6(11):1939–46.

35. Panayides AS, Amini A, Filipovic ND, Sharma A, Tsaftaris SA, Young A, Foran D, Do N, Golemati S, Kurc T, Huang K. AI in medical imaging informatics: current challenges and future directions. *IEEE Journal of Biomedical and Health Informatics.* 2020 May 29;24(7):1837–57.

36. Alhasan M, Hasaneen M. Digital imaging, technologies and artificial intelligence applications during COVID-19 pandemic. *Computerized Medical Imaging and Graphics.* 2021 Jul 1;91:101933.

37. Ahmad Z, Rahim S, Zubair M, Abdul-Ghafar J. Artificial intelligence (AI) in medicine, current applications and future role with special emphasis on its potential and promise in pathology: Present and future impact, obstacles including costs and acceptance among pathologists, practical and philosophical considerations. A comprehensive review. *Diagnostic Pathology.* 2021 Dec;16:1–6.

38. Javaid M, Haleem A, Singh RP, Suman R, Rab S. Significance of machine learning in healthcare: Features, pillars and applications. *International Journal of Intelligent Networks.* 2022 Jan 1;3:58–73.

39. Nayyar A, Gadhavi L, Zaman N. Machine learning in healthcare: review, opportunities and challenges. *Machine Learning and the Internet of Medical Things in Healthcare.* 2021 Jan 1:23–45.

40. Soferman R. The transformative impact of artificial intelligence on healthcare outcomes. *Journal of Clinical Engineering.* 2019 Jul 1;44(3):E1–3.

41. Arvindhan M, Rajeshkumar D, Pal AL. A review of challenges and opportunities in machine learning for healthcare. *Exploratory Data Analytics for Healthcare.* 2021 Dec 23(2021):67–84.

42. Comito C, Falcone D, Forestiero A. AI-Driven clinical decision support: Enhancing disease diagnosis exploiting patients similarity. *IEEE Access.* 2022 Jan 11;10:6878–88.

43. Braun M, Hummel P, Beck S, Dabrock P. Primer on an ethics of AI-based decision support systems in the clinic. *Journal of Medical Ethics.* 2021 Dec 1;47(12):e3–.

44. Edison G. Transforming medical decision-making: A comprehensive review of AI's impact on diagnostics and treatment. *BULLET: Jurnal Multidisiplin Ilmu.* 2023 Aug 23;2(4):1106–14.

45. van Boven JF, Ryan D, Eakin MN, Canonica GW, Barot A, Foster JM, Respiratory effectiveness group. Enhancing respiratory medication adherence: The role of health care professionals and cost-effectiveness considerations. *The Journal of Allergy and Clinical Immunology: In Practice.* 2016 Sep 1;4(5):835–46.

46. Dogheim GM, Hussain A. Patient care through AI-driven remote monitoring: Analyzing the role of predictive models and intelligent alerts in preventive medicine. *Journal of Contemporary Healthcare Analytics.* 2023 Jun 5;7(1):94–110.

47. Javaid M, Haleem A, Singh RP, Suman R, Rab S. Significance of machine learning in healthcare: Features, pillars and applications. *International Journal of Intelligent Networks.* 2022 Jan 1;3:58–73.

48. Sreedevi AG, Harshitha TN, Sugumaran V, Shankar P. Application of cognitive computing in healthcare, cybersecurity, big data and IoT: A literature review. *Information Processing & Management*. 2022 Mar 1;59(2):102888.
49. Zekos GI, Zekos GI. *AI Risk Management. Economics and Law of Artificial Intelligence: Finance, Economic Impacts, Risk Management and Governance*. 2021:233–88.
50. Castaneda C, Nalley K, Mannion C, Bhattacharyya P, Blake P, Pecora A, Goy A, Suh KS. Clinical decision support systems for improving diagnostic accuracy and achieving precision medicine. *Journal of Clinical Bioinformatics*. 2015 Dec;5(1):1–6.
51. Kumar P, Dwivedi YK, Anand A. *Responsible Artificial Intelligence (ai) for Value Formation and Market Performance in Healthcare: The Mediating Role of Patient's Cognitive eEgagement. Information Systems Frontiers*. 2021 Apr 29:1–24.
52. Miyachi K, Mackey TK. hOCBS: A privacy-preserving blockchain framework for healthcare data leveraging an on-chain and off-chain system design. *Information Processing & Management*. 2021 May 1;58(3):102535.
53. Lobo MD. Artificial intelligence in teleradiology: A rapid review of educational and professional contributions. *Handbook of Research on Instructional Technologies in Health Education and Allied Disciplines*. 2023:80–104.
54. Pizzolla I, Aro R, Duez P, De Lièvre B, Briganti G. Integrating artificial intelligence into medical education: Lessons learned from a Belgian initiative. *Journal of Interactive Learning Research*. 2023;34(2):401–24.
55. Bajwa J, Munir U, Nori A, Williams B. Artificial intelligence in healthcare: Transforming the practice of medicine. *Future Healthcare Journal*. 2021 Jul;8(2):e188.
56. Mbunge E, Muchemwa B, Batani J. Sensors and healthcare 5.0: transformative shift in virtual care through emerging digital health technologies. *Global Health Journal*. 2021 Dec 1;5(4):169–77.
57. Albahri AS, Duhaim AM, Fadhel MA, Alnoor A, Baqer NS, Alzubaidi L, Albahri OS, Alamoodi AH, Bai J, Salhi A, Santamaría J. A systematic review of trustworthy and explainable artificial intelligence in healthcare: Assessment of quality, bias risk, and data fusion. *Information Fusion*. 2023 Mar 15.
58. Ali O, Abdelbaki W, Shrestha A, Elbasi E, Alryalat MA, Dwivedi YK. A systematic literature review of artificial intelligence in the healthcare sector: Benefits, challenges, methodologies, and functionalities. *Journal of Innovation & Knowledge*. 2023 Jan 1;8(1):100333.
59. Salmond SW, Echevarria M. Healthcare transformation and changing roles for nursing. *Orthopedic Nursing*. 2017 Jan;36(1):12.
60. Barrett M, Boyne J, Brandts J, Brunner-La Rocca HP, De Maesschalck L, De Wit K, Dixon L, Eurlings C, Fitzsimons D, Golubnitschaja O, Hageman A. Artificial intelligence supported patient self-care in chronic heart failure: A paradigm shift from reactive to predictive, preventive and personalised care. *Epma Journal*. 2019 Dec;10:445–64.
61. Pandya A. *Medical Augmented Reality System for Image-Guided and Robotic Surgery: Development and Surgeon Factors Analysis*. Wayne State University; 2004.
62. Qin Y. *Autonomous Temporal Understanding and State Estimation during Robot-Assisted Surgery*. Doctoral dissertation, California Institute of Technology.
63. Liu R, Gupta S, Patel P. The application of the principles of responsible AI on social media marketing for digital health. *Information Systems Frontiers*. 2021 Sep 13:1–25.

64. Edison G. Transforming medical decision-making: A comprehensive review of AI's impact on diagnostics and treatment. *BULLET: Jurnal Multidisiplin Ilmu.* 2023 Aug 23;2(4):1121–1133.

65. Xie Y, Lu L, Gao F, He SJ, Zhao HJ, Fang Y, Yang JM, An Y, Ye ZW, Dong Z. Integration of artificial intelligence, blockchain, and wearable technology for chronic disease management: A new paradigm in smart healthcare. *Current Medical Science.* 2021 Dec;41:1123–33.

66. Edison G. *The Integration of AI in the Doctor's Toolkit: Enhancing Medical Decision-Making.* BULLET: Jurnal Multidisiplin Ilmu. 2023 Jun 11;2(3):604–13.

67. Javaid M, Haleem A, Singh RP, Suman R, Rab S. Significance of machine learning in healthcare: Features, pillars and applications. *International Journal of Intelligent Networks.* 2022 Jan 1;3:58–73

68. Srivathsa AV, Sadashivappa NM, Hegde AK, Radha S, Mahesh AR, Ammunje DN, Sen D, Theivendren P, Govindaraj S, Kunjiappan S, Pavadai P. A review on artificial intelligence approaches and rational approaches in drug discovery. *Current Pharmaceutical Design.* 2023 Apr 1;29(15):1180–92.

69. Lee D, Yoon SN. Application of artificial intelligence-based technologies in the healthcare industry: Opportunities and challenges. *International Journal of Environmental Research and Public Health.* 2021 Jan;18(1):271.

CHAPTER 5

Biometrics and Data Smart Healthcare System

Ankush Verma, Anam Mohamed Saleem,
Joyce Prabhudas Ranadive, Amit Pratap Singh Chouhan
and Vandana Singh

5.1 INTRODUCTION

5.1.1 Defining Biometrics and Its Role in Healthcare

Biometrics refers to the use and differentiation of physical and personal characteristics. Fingerprints, faces, iris patterns, voice prints, and even good habits like typing or walking in rhythm are examples of these good things. Biometric data is used to identify individuals because no two people have the same biometric characteristics. Biometrics plays an important role in improving safety, accuracy and efficiency in the healthcare industry[1–3]. By adding biometric authentication methods, healthcare systems can provide accurate patient identification, and prevent medical errors, misdiagnoses, and unauthorized access to sensitive medical information[4–5]. Biometric authentication also reduces information and the possibility of spoofing. Biometrics can create personalized treatments. Medical personnel can understand the health and condition of patients by continuously analyzing biometric data for early detection of abnormalities and rapid response. Biometrics can also help create personalized treatment plans, improving the quality of care based on patients' unique biometric characteristics and medical histories[6–9].

5.1.2 Overview of Data Smart Healthcare Systems

Information-intelligent healthcare is driving significant changes in healthcare management and delivery, using the power of information technology to improve patient care, recovery, and improved outcomes. These systems use emerging technologies such as big data analytics, artificial intelligence (AI), Internet of Things (IoT), and machine learning to collect, analyze and interpret large volumes of patient and healthcare data[10–13]. Data smart health systems have the capacity to collect and integrate data from multiple sources,

DOI: 10.1201/9781003430735-5

including medical devices and patient records. By collecting detailed information, doctors can understand patients' health, treatment outcomes and disease patterns[14–16]. Data-intelligent medical systems help personalize medicine by tailoring treatment plans to the patient's specific profile. They make it possible to find genetic markers, biomarkers, and other factors that influence a person's response to various treatments. This self-treatment increases the effectiveness of treatment and reduces negative side effects. Thanks to technology outputs and smartphone applications, patients can take an active role in managing their own health, follow their treatment plans, and access health information. This real-time connection bridges the gap between patients and doctors, fostering collaboration in healthcare management[17–20].

5.1.3 Importance of Integrating Biometrics and Data for Improved Healthcare

The integration of biometrics and data is crucial to support the improvement of healthcare in many areas:

- **Accurate patient identification**: Biometric identifiers such as fingerprints, iris scans and facial recognition provide a reliable and unique way to identify patients and ensure matches with medical data/records. This prevents mistreatment due to wrong instructions and improves patient safety by providing the right treatment and medication[21].

- **Enhanced data security:** To further secure confidential health information, biometric authentication is used. Using biometric authentication to access electronic medical records and other medical systems will protect patient information from unauthorized access and disclosure[22–24].

- **Personalized treatment planning:** The patient can be better understood by connecting biometric data to their medical history. It can assist individualized treatment regimens that consider the patient's particular traits, medical history, and genetic markers, which can produce superior results.

- **Early detection and prevention:** Early identification of health issues and fear is made possible by continuous monitoring of biometric data using wearable technology or sensors. With this strategy, medical professionals may act before the condition worsens, improving outcomes and lowering costs of care.

- **Data-driven insights:** A better knowledge of patient and population health trends and the effects of therapy on outcomes can be achieved by combining biometric data with sophisticated analytics. Planning for research, budget allocation, and public health initiatives can benefit from this knowledge[25–26].

- **Remote monitoring and telemedicine:** By collecting biometric data from wearable devices, the health status of patients can be monitored remotely. By providing virtual counseling based on real biometric data, doctors can improve access to care, especially in remote or underserved areas[27–28].

- **Reduce fraud and identity theft:** Biometric authentication prevents health fraud and identity theft, allowing only individuals to access medical services and services.

5.2 TYPES OF BIOMETRIC DATA IN HEALTHCARE

Various biometric data are used in healthcare to improve patient care, safety and efficiency. These include physical biometrics such as fingerprints, iris patterns and faces, which are unique identifiers for accurate patient identification and access to medical records. Behavioral biometrics, which includes attributes such as beat tempo and music, adds an additional layer of authentication to ensure only authorized personnel can access the editing process. In addition, wearable devices and sensors continuously collect biometric data such as heart rate, body temperature and activity level, enabling early detection of patients, consumption health and insecurity. Integrating genetic information into the field of biometrics can provide insight into a person's susceptibility to certain conditions and their response to treatment, thus promoting personalized medicine[29–30].

5.2.1 Fingerprint Recognition and Its Applications

Physical biometrics or fingerprinting includes identifying specific fingerprint patterns for use in identification and authentication. Due to its accuracy, usability, and non-interference, fingerprint identification is widely utilized in various areas, including healthcare[31–32]. The use of fingerprinting in medicine has various advantages:

- **Patient identification**: Using fingerprints to identify patients and tying them to medical records helps to ensure that the appropriate person is receiving care. Additionally, it raises the level of care and patient safety while avoiding medical errors.

- **Access to health records**: Secure access to electronic health records (EHRs) and private patient data is made possible through fingerprint authentication. Patient information is kept secret and complies with laws like HIPAA since only authorized healthcare practitioners may access it.

- **Time and attendance tracking:** In healthcare institutions, fingerprint devices may be used to monitor staff attendance and to record their working hours for scheduling and payment.

- **Blood and drug administration:** Fingertips can be used to improve a patient's blood tests to ensure the blood is drawn correctly. It can also be used in the treatment of drug addiction.

- **Patient monitoring:** The fingerprint of wearable devices can allow continuous monitoring of patients, help manage patients in rural areas, and help detect health problems at an early stage.

- **Access control:** Fingerprint authentication against restricted access areas in medical facilities, preventing access to sensitive areas such as operating theatres, diagnostic facilities and medical facilities.

5.2.2 Iris and Retinal Scanning for Patient Identification

Iris and retina scans are advanced biometric technologies that have made significant advances in patient identification in healthcare. Iris scanning uses near-infrared light to detect special patterns in the color of the eye, called the iris. Similarly, a retinal scan focuses on the specific pattern of blood vessels in the retina[33–35]. Because of the inconsistency of facial features, the two methods provide consistency and confidence in patient identification. Iris and retina scanning has many benefits for medical facilities. Non-invasive structures improve patient comfort and hygiene since they avoid physical touch and suffering. Technology decreases the danger of misinformation and improves patient safety, particularly in critical situations such as treatment and medication or medical information sensitivity[36].

5.2.3 Voice Recognition and Speech Analysis in Healthcare

Speech analysis and recognition are now crucial medical technologies that have a wide range of uses for bettering patient care and diagnosis. With the use of this technology, voice can now be converted into digital data, facilitating communication between patients, medical records, and even other medical records. By identifying changes in voice, voice, and speech patterns, the speech scanning tool can assist in the early detection of neurological and mental illnesses[37–38].

5.2.4 Facial Recognition for Patient Authentication

As a secure and reliable method of identifying patients, facial recognition technology has several advantages for the healthcare industry. This technology enables healthcare organizations to improve patient identification procedures' accuracy and efficiency, lowering the risk of abuse and ensuring the right care is given. It does this by identifying distinctive faces and patterns[39]. Using biometric technologies such as facial recognition and biometrics, doctors can quickly and accurately match a patient's electronic medical records, medications, and procedures with medical condition plans. Technology can also streamline the management of operations and reduce cases of theft or fraud in healthcare facilities.

5.2.5 Heart Rate Variability and Biometric Monitoring

Heart rate variability (HRV) has received widespread attention as an important biometric parameter in the monitoring and evaluation of a person's brain function and general health. HRV refers to the short-term variability of sequential heart rates and reflects the changes and activity of the cardiovascular system against different physiological and environmental stressors. Biometric monitoring using HRV analysis has applications in many areas, including healthcare, exercise, and stress management[40]. By capturing changes in heart rate patterns, HRV can provide insight into conditions like heart disease, stress, and even mental illness[41]. Equipped with advanced wearables and HRV sensors, mobile apps help with real-time monitoring and analysis, allowing people to track their health and create conscious lifestyles.

5.3 ADVANTAGES OF BIOMETRICS IN HEALTHCARE

The use of biometrics in healthcare is growing because it has several advantages that enhance patient care, safety, and effectiveness. The use of physiological or behavioral signals provided by biometric technology, such as fingerprint, iris scanning, and face recognition, for patient identification, identification, and access control is possible. Increased security for patient data, medical records, and sensitive hospitals is a significant advantage that helps prevent unauthorized access and potential exposure[42]. The patient enrollment procedure is also made simpler by biometric authentication, which further cuts down on waiting times and administrative work. This improves overall patient happiness and experience[43].

5.3.1 Enhanced Patient Identification and Safety

As patient privacy and safety are essential components of modern healthcare, increasing patient identity and safety is a crucial concern. The manual input of individual information is frequently used in current patient identification systems, which leads to errors and instability[44]. Biometric technology can help with these issues since it gives precise and one-of-a-kind information about the patient. The accuracy of patient identification and verification is increased by biometric technology including fingerprints, faces, and iris patterns[45]. Healthcare organizations may develop strong and trustworthy patient identification systems that assist in lowering medical mistakes, permit unauthorized access, and release medical information by utilizing biometric technologies.

5.3.2 Reducing Medical Errors and Misdiagnoses

Reducing medical mistakes and misdiagnosis has emerged as the most pressing issue in modern medicine. Data input and identification are commonly used in patient identification operations; this is a mistake that leads to medical errors. Biometrics has emerged as a potentially viable answer to this issue[46]. These statistics enable clinicians to deliver correct medical information, treatment plans, and drugs, lowering the likelihood of unneeded management or intervention. By lowering the amount of misdiagnoses, health care institutions can enhance patient safety, quality of treatment, and overall care[47].

5.4 CHALLENGES AND CONSIDERATIONS

The use of technologies such as biometrics and electronic health records (EHR) in healthcare presents challenges and issues that need to be carefully addressed[48]. A key challenge is the need to balance security and privacy concerns with the benefits of improved patient identification and access to information. While biometrics provides better authentication, concerns about data breaches and misuse of biometric data still need to be carefully managed[49]. The integration of new technologies requires good training of doctors to ensure that they are used effectively and that no mistakes are made.

5.4.1 Privacy Concerns and Data Protection

Privacy concerns arise from misuse, unauthorized access or destruction of this information. In the context of biometrics, the potential was stolen for certain physiological or behavioral traits and biometric data used to identify the problem of long-term stability of these indicators. By prioritizing privacy concerns and enforcing strong data protection policies, healthcare organizations can leverage technology while protecting patient privacy and data security[50–51].

5.4.2 Biometric Accuracy

Biometric technologies such as fingerprint recognition, iris scanning and facial recognition hold great promise in improving patient identity and security in healthcare systems. A major concern is the accuracy and error rate of biometric measurements. Biometric systems are also vulnerable to flaws and vulnerabilities. False positives occur when the system does not correctly identify the person as an authorized user, resulting in unauthorized access. Efforts to improve biometric accuracy include advances in technology, advanced imaging techniques, and machine learning algorithms[52–53].

These measures are designed to strengthen the biometric system and reduce errors. It is important for healthcare organizations to use biometric solutions along with other authentication and security measures to create effective security and stability.

5.4.3 Ethical Implications of Biometric Data Usage

The use of biometric data in healthcare has important implications that need to be carefully evaluated. Biometric technologies such as fingerprint and face scanning naturally capture a person's physical or behavioral characteristics. Consent is an important ethical issue.

Another ethical consideration is the potential negative consequences such as data breaches or unauthorized access to information[54–55]. Healthcare organizations are responsible for implementing security measures to protect biometric data from cyberattacks and unauthorized use.

5.5 INTEGRATION OF BIOMETRICS WITH DATA SMART HEALTHCARE SYSTEMS

The integration of biometrics and data-intelligent healthcare holds great promise for improving patient care, safety and efficiency. Data-intelligent healthcare uses advanced analytics and artificial intelligence to process and analyze large volumes of patient data, making more informed decisions, medical decisions and personalized treatment plans. Healthcare providers can assist patients achieve better results while delivering a better and safer patient experience by merging biometrics with data intelligence[56–57].

A ground-breaking method of using technology to enhance patient health and well-being is the use of biometrics for real-time monitoring and health prediction. Doctors can comprehend a patient's health, trace changes, and spot anomalies thanks to continuous monitoring. Machine learning algorithms can analyze biometric data in real-time to foretell potential diseases or issues and alert medical professionals[58–59]. For example, changes in biomarkers may indicate an increased risk of cardiovascular disease or chronic disease.

5.6 DATA SECURITY AND PRIVACY MEASURES

Data security and privacy are paramount when integrating biometrics into healthcare. To address these issues, healthcare organizations should implement security measures, encryption procedures, and access controls to ensure the confidentiality, knowledge, and integrity of biometric data[60–61].

Encrypting and securely storing biometric data is an essential part of maintaining patient privacy and data integrity in healthcare systems. To protect this data from unauthorized access and destruction, strong encryption is used while the data is transmitted and stored[62–63].

5.7 SMART HEALTHCARE APPLICATIONS

Intelligent healthcare applications powered by innovations such as the Internet of Things (IoT), artificial intelligence (AI) and data analytics are transforming health and patient outcomes. These applications include a variety of solutions that improve patient care, diagnosis, monitoring and productivity. IoT-enabled devices such as wearable fitness trackers and remote patient monitors collect real-time health data, allowing doctors to monitor patients' vital signs and chronic illnesses. These smart medical apps have many benefits. It enables patients to play an important role in health management, increases patient participation and allows for early intervention [64–65]. The integration of these technologies can improve health by streamlining processes, reducing administrative burdens and improving resource allocation.

5.7.1 Remote Patient Monitoring with Biometric Sensors

Remote patient monitoring with biometric sensors has revolutionized healthcare using technology to improve patient care and management. These sensors can capture vital signs, heart rate, blood pressure, and other biometric data related to a better understanding of the patient's health. Integrating biometric sensors with remote patient monitoring has many benefits. Doctors can care for patients with chronic illnesses, diagnose poor or ill-health, and potentially prevent hospitalization or problems with timely intervention. Patients benefit from greater involvement in health management when they receive feedback and alerts based on biometric data, which increases understanding of support and adherence to treatment plans[66–67].

5.7.2 Biometric Drug Delivery Systems

Systems for biometric medication administration offer a way to enhance patient safety and drug management in healthcare settings. To guarantee that the right patient receives medication, these systems employ biometric verification, such as fingerprint or face recognition. There are several benefits of using biometrics in medicine delivery. First off, guaranteeing that only authorized patients are injected eliminates the potential of a mistake injection or medication mixing. A second benefit of biometric identification is that it lowers the risk of theft and drug usage[68]. Additionally, the system can document drug monitoring and administration, giving medical professionals supervision and transparency.

5.7.3 Biometric Authentication for Telemedicine and E-health Platforms

Platforms for telemedicine and e-health may now be secured and authenticated using biometrics. These technologies, such as voice, face, and fingerprint identification, offer reliable and efficient means to identify patients during medical operations. The possibility of mobile impersonation is decreased thanks to biometric authentication, which also improves the security of patient data. Multiple difficulties are addressed when biometric identification is integrated with telemedicine and e-Health systems. First, the convenience of self-identification enables patients to access their medical records and attend virtual appointments with ease and security. Second, by removing the need to memorize complicated passwords or shared credentials, biometric systems improve patient privacy. Finally, it executes virtual care, offers user experience to promote patient involvement, and regulates patient care standards[69].

5.8 FUTURE TRENDS AND INNOVATIONS

5.8.1 Advances in Biometrics in Healthcare

Biometric technology advancements are revolutionizing healthcare by offering fresh approaches to patient identification, data security, and individualized treatment. Biometric systems like fingerprint, iris, and face identification are becoming smarter, more precise, and simpler to use. smart health records (EHRs) and smart phones are increasingly connected with technologies, enabling secure patient visits and connecting patients to medical information.

5.8.2 Wearable Biometric Devices for Continuous Health Monitoring

Wearable biometric devices have evolved into crucial instruments for continuous health monitoring by providing people with information about their diseases and conditions. These gadgets include smartwatches, fitness and health trackers, and blood oxygen monitors, which allow users to monitor events such as heart rate, sleep, exercise, and even blood oxygen levels. Biometric gadgets can help people make more educated decisions about their health, wellbeing, and lifestyle by combining modern sensors and analytical data. Wearable biometric devices allow continuous monitoring, which is especially useful for detecting changes in health. The technology alerts users and service providers to potential problems so that they may respond and prevent them as soon as possible.

The data generated by these wearables may be used to manage chronic diseases, monitor health, and promote behavioral changes that will benefit the environment[70].

5.8.3 Personalized Medicine Based on Biometric and Genetic Data

Wearable biometric sensors that provide information on a person's condition and pain have developed into crucial instruments for ongoing medical treatment. Smartwatches, fitness trackers, and health trackers are some of the gadgets that enable users to keep an eye on things like heart rate, sleep, exercise, and even blood oxygen levels. By combining cutting-edge sensors and analytical data, biometric devices can provide a more comprehensive understanding of a person's health, empowering users to make decisions about their health, wellbeing, and lifestyle. For the early detection of changes in health, the continuous monitoring offered by wearable biometric equipment is particularly helpful. The technology alerts consumers and service providers to possible problems so they can react quickly and take preventive measures. These wearable gadgets' data may be used to treat chronic illnesses, track health, and encourage general behavioral improvements[71].

5.9 JUSTICE AND LEGITIMACY

5.9.1 Consent Convention on the Collection and Use of Biometric Data

Consent plays an important role in the collection and use of biometric data in healthcare. Patients sign a consent form to confirm that they are aware of how their biometric data will be gathered, kept, utilized, and shared. The goal of data gathering, any possible advantages, and any dangers or privacy issues should all be understood by patients[72]. Patients should be informed in a simple and straightforward manner about the biometrics being used, the precise data being gathered, the individuals having access to the data, and the privacy safeguards. The procedure for withdrawing consent should be explained to patients, along with their right to do so.

5.9.2 Evaluating the Benefits of Biometrics and Patient Autonomy

An essential part of healthcare is assessing the advantages of biometrics and patient autonomy. The gathering and utilization of physical or behavioral data is a component of biometric solutions, which enhance clinical procedures, patient identity, data security, and clinical workflow. By weighing the advantages of biometrics against the patient's right to control their data, it is possible to respect patient privacy. The challenge is to ensure that the use of biometric technology does not violate patient rights and privacy[73]. Physicians should clearly explain to patients the purpose, potential, and impact of collecting and using biometric data so that patients can make an informed decision about participation.

5.9.3 Legal Frameworks Governing Biometric Data in Healthcare

Legal frameworks play an important role in regulating the collection, storage and use of biometric data in healthcare. Biometric information is sensitive and unique; requires good controls to protect patient privacy, ensure data security and maintain ethical standards. In healthcare, regulations such as the Health Insurance Portability and Accountability Act (HIPAA) in the US, the General Data Protection Regulation (GDPR) in the EU, and many other national data protection laws contain legal provisions regarding the use of biometrics[74]. This legal framework outlines the requirements for consent, disclosure of breached information, access control and information sharing.

5.10 CONCLUSION

As a result, the integration of biometrics and data-intelligent healthcare systems is important in improving healthcare and patient management. Precision medicine, cutting-edge patient care, and increased productivity are all made possible by the seamless integration of sophisticated biometrics with data analytics, artificial intelligence, and the Internet of Things. Biometric technology, such as fingerprint, facial recognition, and heart rate monitoring, offers precise and secure patient identification, lowers medical mistakes, and enhances patient experiences. Through wearable devices, this technology may also offer continuous healthcare and real-time monitoring, enticing patients to take part in healthcare management, healthy drinking, and early health abnormality detection. Clinical judgment, individualized treatment plans, and preventive measures can all benefit from the integration of biometric and cognitive data. By drawing valuable conclusions from biometric data, the data analysis process aids monitoring and risk assessments. The security of telemedicine and e-Health platforms is also increased by biometric authentication, ensuring that patient information is kept private and only available to those with the proper authorization. However, it is crucial to understand and deal with ethical concerns including patient autonomy, data privacy, and permission. Future applications in healthcare will increase as biometrics and data analytics continue to advance. These innovations have the power to completely alter clinical practise, treatment plans, and diagnostics. However, in order to effectively use the therapeutic potential of biometric and data smart technologies while preserving patient rights and privacy, compliance, and contact with patients are crucial. Ultimately, the combination of biometrics and data smart healthcare will lead to more patient, efficient and effective healthcare.

REFERENCES

1. Vacca J. R. *Biometric Technologies and Verification Systems.* 2007 Mar 16, Elsevier.
2. De Keyser A, Bart Y, Gu X, Liu S. Q, Robinson S. G, Kannan P. K. Opportunities and challenges of using biometrics for business: Developing a research agenda. *Journal of Business Research.* 2021 Nov 1;136:52–62.
3. Sun Y, Zhang M, Sun Z, Tan T. Demographic analysis from biometric data: Achievements, challenges, and new frontiers. *IEEE Transactions on Pattern Analysis and Machine Intelligence.* 2017 Feb 14;40(2):332–51.
4. Mason J, Dave R, Chatterjee P, Graham-Allen I, Esterline A, Roy K. An investigation of biometric authentication in the healthcare environment. *Array.* 2020 Dec 1;8:100042.
5. Segun O. F, Olawale F. B. Healthcare data breaches: Biometric technology to the rescue. *International Research Journal of Engineering and Technology.* 2017 Nov;4(11):946–50.
6. Mason J, Dave R, Chatterjee P, Graham-Allen I, Esterline A, Roy K. An investigation of biometric authentication in the healthcare environment. *Array.* 2020 Dec 1;8:100042.
7. Kumar U, Tripathi E, Tripathi S. P, Gupta K. K. Deep learning for healthcare biometrics. In *Design and Implementation of Healthcare Biometric Systems* 2019. (pp. 73–108). IGI Global.

8. Singh AK, Anand A, Lv Z, Ko H, Mohan A. A survey on healthcare data: A security perspective. *ACM Transactions on Multimidia Computing Communications and Applications.* 2021 May 17;17(2s):1–26.

9. Sharma N, Kaushik I, Bhushan B, Gautam S, Khamparia A. Applicability of WSN and biometric models in the field of healthcare. In *Deep Learning Strategies for Security Enhancement in Wireless Sensor Networks* 2020. (pp. 304–329). IGI Global.

10. Sharma A, Sharma V, Jaiswal M, Wang H. C, Jayakody D. N, Basnayaka C. M, Muthanna A. Recent trends in AI-based intelligent sensing. *Electronics.* 2022 May 23;11(10):1661.

11. Ma R, Liu B. Analysis of factors influencing the development of mHealth innovation based on data mining algorithms. *Mathematical Problems in Engineering.* 2022 Aug 30;2022.

12. Thakur C, Gupta S. Multi-Agent system applications in health care: A survey. In *Multi Agent Systems: Technologies and Applications Towards Human-Centered.* 2022 Apr 26 (pp. 139–171). Singapore: Springer Nature Singapore.

13. Dridi A, Sassi S, Faiz S. A smart IoT platform for personalized healthcare monitoring using semantic technologies. In *2017 IEEE 29th International Conference on Tools with Artificial Intelligence (ICTAI).* 2017 Nov 6 (pp. 1198–1203). IEEE.

14. Manogaran G, Thota C, Lopez D, Sundarasekar R. Big data security intelligence for healthcare industry 4.0. In: Thames, L., Schaefer, D. (eds) *Cybersecurity for Industry 4.0. Springer Series in Advanced Manufacturing.* 2017 (pp. 103–1026). Cham: Springer. https://doi.org/10.1007/978-3-319-50660-9_5

15. Dwivedi R, Mehrotra D, Chandra S. Potential of internet of medical things (IoMT) applications in building a smart healthcare system: A systematic review. *Journal of Oral Biology and Craniofacial Research.* 2022 Mar 1;12(2):302–18.

16. Cai Q, Wang H, Li Z, Liu X. A survey on multimodal data-driven smart healthcare systems: Approaches and applications. *IEEE Access.* 2019 Sep 13;7:133583–99.

17. Srivastava J, Routray S, Ahmad S, Waris M. M. Internet of medical things (IoMT)-based smart healthcare system: Trends and progress. *Computational Intelligence and Neuroscience.* 2022 Jul 16;2022.

18. Rani S, Chauhan M, Kataria A, Khang A. *IoT Equipped Intelligent Distributed Framework for Smart Healthcare Systems. arXiv preprint arXiv:2110.04997.* 2021 Oct 11.

19. Vaiyapuri T, Binbusayyis A, Varadarajan V. Security, privacy and trust in IoMT enabled smart healthcare system: A systematic review of current and future trends. *International Journal of Advanced Computer Science and Applications.* 2021;12(2):731–737.

20. Sahu M. L, Atulkar M, Ahirwal M. K. IOT-based smart healthcare system: a review on constituent technologies. *Journal of Circuits, Systems and Computers.* 2021 Sep 15;30(11):2130008.

21. Nigam D, Patel S. N, Raj Vincent P. M, Srinivasan K, Arunmozhi S. Biometric authentication for intelligent and privacy-preserving healthcare systems. *Journal of Healthcare Engineering.* 2022 Mar 24;2022.

22. Karunarathne S. M, Saxena N, Khan M. K. Security and privacy in IoT smart healthcare. *IEEE Internet Computing.* 2021 Jan 18;25(4):37–48.

23. Shi S, He D, Li L, Kumar N, Khan M. K, Choo K. K. Applications of blockchain in ensuring the security and privacy of electronic health record systems: A survey. *Computers & security.* 2020 Oct 1;97:101966.

24. Pussewalage H. S, Oleshchuk V. A. Privacy preserving mechanisms for enforcing security and privacy requirements in E-health solutions. *International Journal of Information Management.* 2016 Dec 1;36(6):1161–73.

25. Pramanik P. K, Pal S, Mukhopadhyay M. Healthcare big data: A comprehensive overview. *Research Anthology on Big Data Analytics, Architectures, and Applications.* 2022:119–47.

26. Morgan V, Birtus M, Zauskova A. Medical internet of things-based healthcare systems, wearable biometric sensors, and personalized clinical care in remotely monitoring and caring for confirmed or suspected COVID-19 patients. *American Journal of Medical Research.* 2021;8(1):81–90.

27. Kalid N, Zaidan A. A, Zaidan B. B, Salman O. H, Hashim M, Muzammil H. J. Based real time remote health monitoring systems: A review on patients prioritization and related "big data" using body sensors information and communication technology. *Journal of medical systems.* 2018 Feb;42:1–30.

28. Letafati M, Otoum S. On the privacy and security for e-health services in the metaverse: An overview. *Ad Hoc Networks.* 2023 Aug 2;150:103262.

29. Mathew P. S, Pillai A. S, Palade V. Applications of IoT in healthcare. In: Sangaiah, A., Thangavelu, A., Meenakshi Sundaram, V. (eds) *Cognitive Computing for Big Data Systems Over IoT.* Lecture Notes on Data Engineering and Communications Technologies. 2018; 14: 263–288. Cham: Springer, https://doi.org/10.1007/978-3-319-70688-7_11

30. Dunn J, Runge R, Snyder M. Wearables and the medical revolution. *Personalized Medicine.* 2018 Sep;15(5):429–48.

31. Sharif M, Raza M, Shah J. H, Yasmin M, Fernandes SL. An overview of biometrics methods. *Handbook of Multimedia Information Security: Techniques and Applications.* 2019:4:15–35.

32. Hamidi H. An approach to develop the smart health using internet of things and authentication based on biometric technology. *Future Generation Computer Systems.* 2019 Feb 1;91:434–49.

33. Buciu I, Gacsadi A. Biometrics systems and technologies: A survey. *International Journal of Computers Communications & Control.* 2016 Mar 24;11(3):315–30.

34. Sabhanayagam T, Venkatesan V. P, Senthamaraikannan K. A comprehensive survey on various biometric systems. *International Journal of Applied Engineering Research.* 2018;13(5):2276–97.

35. Hung T. C, Tri N. T, Minh H. N. An Enhanced security for government base on multifactor biometric authentication. *International Journal of Computer Networks & Communications (IJCNC).* 2016;8:55–72.

36. Esteva A, Chou K, Yeung S, Naik N, Madani A, Mottaghi A, Liu Y, Topol E, Dean J, Socher R. Deep learning-enabled medical computer vision. *NPJ Digital Medicine.* 2021 Jan 8;4(1):5.

37. Smith, A., Haider, H., Perez-Carrillo, G. J., Tsanas, A., Little, M. A. Objective assessment of depressive symptoms with machine learning and speech signal processing techniques. *Proceedings of the IEEE International Conference on Acoustics, Speech, and Signal Processing (ICASSP).* 2019 6854–6858.

38. Johnson, M. E., Varnet, L., Beck, J. G. Acoustic features of speech in Parkinson's disease: A meta-analysis and meta-regression of speaker characteristics. *Journal of Speech, Language, and Hearing Research.* 2020;63(5):1492–1505.

39. Smith, J. K., Johnson, L. M., Williams, R. S. Facial recognition technology for secure patient authentication in healthcare environments. *Journal of Medical Informatics*. 2021;42:101–110.

40. Thayer, J. F., Yamamoto, S. S., Brosschot, J. F. The relationship of autonomic imbalance, heart rate variability and cardiovascular disease risk factors. *International Journal of Cardiology*. 2010;141(2):122–131.

41. Quintana, D. S., Heathers, J. A., Kemp, A. H., Quinn, C. R. Guidelines for reporting articles on psychiatry and heart rate variability (GRAPH): Recommendations to advance research communication. *Translational Psychiatry*. 2016;6(5):e803.

42. Khan, N. A., Qureshi, K. N., Raza, N. A. Biometric data in healthcare: A survey of recent trends and state-of-the-art applications. *IEEE Access*. 2020;8:186992–187020.

43. Ali, S., Haq, T. U., Raza, A. A framework for biometric-based healthcare systems: Issues, challenges, and opportunities. *IEEE Access*. 2019;7:142136–142153.

44. Ciompi, F., Kallenberg, M., Akerkar, R., Chung, K., Scholten, E. T., et al. Towards automatic pulmonary nodule management in lung cancer screening with deep learning. *Scientific Reports*. 2020;10(1):1–14.

45. Kharrazi, H., Anzaldi, L. J., Hernandez, L., Davison, A., Boyd, C. M., Leff, B., Kim, H. The value of unstructured electronic health record data in geriatric syndrome case identification. *Journal of the American Geriatrics Society*. 2019;67(11):2312–2319.

46. Ciompi, F., Kallenberg, M., Akerkar, R., Chung, K., Scholten, E. T., et al. Towards automatic pulmonary nodule management in lung cancer screening with deep learning. *Scientific Reports*. 2020;10(1):1–14.

47. Kharrazi, H., Anzaldi, L. J., Hernandez, L., Davison, A., Boyd, C. M., Leff, B., Kim, H. The value of unstructured electronic health record data in geriatric syndrome case identification. *Journal of the American Geriatrics Society*. 2019;67(11):2312–2319.

48. Yoo, S. K., Kim, J. W., Kim, H. E. Security enhancement for biometric-based electronic health record system. *Healthcare Informatics Research*. 2019;25(2):123–129.

49. Mandel, J. C., Kreda, D. A., Mandl, K. D., Kohane, I. S. Ramifications of the 21st century cures Act for clinical research and patient care. *JAMA*. 2020;323(11):1021–1022.

50. Kuo, T. T., Ohno-Machado, L., Ohno-Machado, L. Model-Driven privacy engineering for health data systems. *JAMA*. 2020;323(22):2239–2240.

51. Yoo, S. K., Kim, J. W., Kim, H. E. Security enhancement for biometric-based electronic health record system. *Healthcare Informatics Research*. 2019;25(2):123–129.

52. Jain, A. K., Ross, A., Prabhakar, S. An introduction to biometric recognition. *IEEE Transactions on Circuits and Systems for Video Technology*. 2004;14(1):4–20.

53. Marasco, E., Roli, F., Campisi, P. Image quality qssessment for fake biometric detection: Application to Iris, fingerprint, and face recognition. *IEEE Transactions on Information Forensics and Security*. 2016;11(10):2235–2250.

54. Hall, J. W., Goss, J. R., Giordano, J. Biometrics, ethics and medical practice. *European Journal of Clinical Investigation*. 2017;47(1):3–10.

55. Yoo, S. K., Kim, J. W., Kim, H. E. Security enhancement for biometric-based electronic health record system. *Healthcare Informatics Research*. 2019;25(2):123–129.

56. Khan, N. A., Qureshi, K. N., Raza, N. A. Biometric data in healthcare: A survey of recent trends and state-of-the-art applications. *IEEE Access*. 2020;8:186992–187020.

57. Topalovic, D., Seifert, C. M., Perera, C. Biometric data analytics: Understanding health from data through modeling, prediction, and decision making. *IEEE Engineering in Medicine and Biology Magazine.* 2019;38(6):45–51.

58. Kharrazi, H., Anzaldi, L. J., Hernandez, L., Davison, A., Boyd, C. M., Leff, B., Kim, H. The value of unstructured electronic health record data in geriatric syndrome case identification. *Journal of the American Geriatrics Society.* 2019;67(11):2312–2319.

59. Khan, N. A., Qureshi, K. N., Raza, N. A. Biometric data in healthcare: A survey of recent trends and state-of-the-art applications. *IEEE Access.* 2020;8:186992–187020.

60. Batko K, Ślęzak A. The use of Big Data Analytics in healthcare. *Journal of Big Data.* 2022;9(1):3–24. DOI: 10.1186/s40537-021-00553-4. Epub 2022 Jan 6. PMID: 35013701; PMCID: PMC8733917.

61. Yoo, S. K., Kim, J. W., Kim, H. E. Security enhancement for biometric-based electronic health record system. *Healthcare Informatics Research.* 2019;25(2):123–129.

62. Yoo, S. K., Kim, J. W., Kim, H. E. Security enhancement for biometric-based electronic health record system. *Healthcare Informatics Research.* 2019;25(2):123–129.

63. Akinyelu, A. O., Awodele, O. Cryptography techniques for healthcare information systems security: A review. *Heliyon.* 2021;7(1):e05963.

64. Baker, Stephanie B., Xiang, Wei, et Atkinson, Ian. Internet of things for smart healthcare: Technologies, challenges, and opportunities. *Ieee Access,* 2017;5:26521–26544.

65. Choi, E., Schuetz, A., Stewart, W. F., Sun, J. Using recurrent neural network models for early detection of heart failure onset. *Journal of the American Medical Informatics Association.* 2017;24(2):361–370.

66. Islam, M. R., Islam, R., Ayon, S. I., Uddin, M. M., Mahmud, M., Reaz, M. B. A review on wearable technology: A multidisciplinary view. *Journal of Ambient Intelligence and Humanized Computing.* 2021;12(2):1843–1869.

67. Brooks, G. C., Lee, W. H., Burkart, D. C., Vittinghoff, E. Accuracy of a wrist-worn wearable device for monitoring heart rates in hospital inpatients: A prospective observational study. *Journal of Medical Internet Research.* 2017;19(11):e372.

68. Prakash, P., Sahoo, G. C., Meenakshi, Kumar, R. P. Biometric authentication and medication compliance-a new approach in mHealth. In *Proceedings of the International Conference on Inventive Computing and Informatics (ICICI)* 2017. (pp. 717–721). Springer.

69. Hu, J., Liu, J., Wu, Z. Two-factor authentication scheme with biometric and OTP for mobile health telemedicine system. *IEEE Access.* 2021;9:36082–36094.

70. Liu, S., Jiang, W., Yi, X., Ma, X., Han, Z., Wang, Y., Ma, C. An overview of wearables and IoT in healthcare. *IEEE Internet of Things Journal.* 2020;8(12):11477–11493.

71. Hamburg, M. A., Collins, F. S. The path to personalized medicine. *New England Journal of Medicine.* 2010;363(4):301–304.

72. Al-khaldi, Y. M., Alghamdi, B. A., Alghamdi, F. A., Alqahtani, M. A., Alsufayan, B. S. The Role of Informed Consent in Biometric Data Collection. *SN Comprehensive Clinical Medicine.* 2021;3(4):1735–1742.

73. Bhatia, A., Gaur, A. B., Kumar, V. Biometrics in healthcare: patient identification and beyond. *Biometrics in Healthcare.* 2020;237.

74. Goldstein, M. S., Bavasso, M. US biometric privacy laws: Current developments. *International Data Privacy Law.* 2020;10(1):79–95.

CHAPTER 6

Analysing the Ascendant Trend of Veganism: A Comprehensive Study on the Shift towards Sustainable Dietary Choices

Shikha Bhagat, Shilpa Sarvani Ravi and Rashmi Rai

6.1 INTRODUCTION

A vegan is someone who generally avoids using animal products and does not consume any food made from animals, often for ethical, spiritual, or health-related reasons. A vegan doesn't really even use anything produced from leather, feathers, fur, etc. Vegans are people who don't eat meat and aren't allowed to consume anything that has been subjected to animal testing (Smith, 2020; Brown & Jones, 2021). It has emerged as a prominent social and dietary movement that has gained significant traction in recent years. With its roots deeply embedded in ethical considerations, environmental concerns, and personal health, veganism represents a lifestyle choice that aims to exclude the consumption and use of animal products in all aspects of life (Kwiatkowska et al., 2022).

Furthermore, personal health has become a key motivating factor for individuals embracing veganism. A well-planned vegan diet can provide an array of essential nutrients, including fibre, vitamins, minerals, and antioxidants. A balanced vegan diet, when properly planned, has been found to have many health advantages, including lowering the chance of developing chronic conditions including heart disease, diabetes, and some types of cancer (Fox & Ward, 2008). In order to create a final product that resembles actual meat and may be used as a meat substitute, vegan products are typically manufactured with soy protein, mushrooms, rice, lentils, and wheat gluten (Miller, 2022).

DOI: 10.1201/9781003430735-6

There are various reasons why someone can decide to become vegan:

- To cease funding the meat business while they continue to horrendously butcher our farm animals.
- For the sake of health (eating meat can lead to heart disease, diabetes, and high cholesterol).
- To protect the environment (factory farming is one of the main causes of global warming).
- Concerns regarding the composition of meat owing to additions and chemicals (most of us have no idea what is in it).

Additionally, there are always people who act in a certain way because it is the norm.

The emphasis on whole plant foods in a vegan diet also encourages a higher intake of fibre and lower consumption of saturated fats, contributing to overall well-being (Fresán & Sabaté, 2019). Quantitative research explains how often or how many behave in a certain way. Qualitative research has no substitute as it broadens or deepens research understanding of how things came to be the way they are in the social world.

Twitter (now known as X), a well-known social networking platform, can interact with its followers by sending them quick messages known as tweets. It is a helpful tool for businesses, individuals, and organisations to interact with their audiences and take part in discussions about important topics. It has over 330 million active users globally each month. Users may quickly find and join conversations on a variety of topics because of Twitter's distinctive features, including hashtags and retweets. As a result, there are now vibrant communities on the platform where users can interact and exchange ideas with people who have similar interests. For companies and organisations trying to develop their brand and interact with their target audience, Twitter is a potent tool (Twitter, 2021). Businesses may develop a devoted following on the platform and promote themselves as thought leaders in their field by publishing pertinent material, answering customer questions, and taking part in pertinent conversations. Hence Twitter can be considered a most influential platform and gives an opportunity to every user to shout out their thoughts. With this as a key advantage in Twitter, exploratory research can be conducted using thematic, sentimental and word cloud analysis. These potential perspectives of the users can be identified, accessed and measured accurately by using NVivo. NVivo was developed by QSR International for qualitative data analysis to examine the content and narrative analysis (QSR International, 2021).

Scopus is the largest Abstract and Indexing database worldwide. It is important to bear in mind that the database is continuously growing at ~8% CAGR (Compound Annual Growth Rate) (Elsevier, 2021). Currently, the database contains over 81 million records. Investigation of Scopus data files can examine the trend of research and the outcomes of published papers and serve as an exploratory qualitative study.

6.1.1 Evolution of Veganism

The evolution of veganism is a fascinating subject that showcases the development and transformation of the vegan movement over time. Here is an overview of the key stages and milestones in the evolution of veganism:

Origins and early influences: The roots of veganism can be traced back to ancient civilisations, where certain religious and philosophical traditions advocated for vegetarian or plant-based diets. In 1945, the word "vegan" was first used by Donald Watson and a group of vegetarians who formed the Vegan Society in the United Kingdom. They adopted a lifestyle that forbade any usage of animal products, such as dairy and eggs, in an effort to set themselves apart from vegetarians.

Ethical foundations and animal rights: Animal rights awareness and ethical issues have long been at the core of veganism. A wider awareness of and activism for veganism as a strategy to enhance animal welfare was sparked by influential publications like "Animal Liberation" by Singer (1975) and "The Sexual Politics of Meat" by Adams (1990), which furthered the ethical arguments against animal exploitation.

Environmental concerns: The environmental advantages of veganism have received more attention in recent years due to growing public awareness of environmental challenges including climate change and resource depletion (Scarborough et al., 2014; Aleksandrowicz et al., 2016). Veganism's contribution to lowering greenhouse gas emissions, deforestation, and water pollution has been noted in research on the environmental effects of animal agriculture, notably the United Nations Livestock's Long Shadow (2008) report.

Health and wellness: The health benefits associated with a well-planned vegan diet have also played a significant role in the evolution of veganism (Dinu et al., 2017; Tuso et al., 2013). According to scientific studies, a balanced vegan diet can offer all the essential nutrients while lowering the chance of developing certain chronic conditions like heart disease, obesity, and type 2 diabetes (Bhagat and Ravi, 2018). Due to this evidence, plant-based diets are becoming more and more popular among people who want to enhance their health (Craig & Mangels, 2009; Huang et al., 2016).

Mainstream acceptance and industry response: The mainstream culture has become more aware of and accepting of veganism. Due to rising consumer demand and market trends, vegan options and goods are now substantially more readily available in grocery stores, eateries, and fast-food chains (Harrison et al., 2018; Mintel, 2021). The growth of social media and online networks has also aided in the spread of veganism by allowing people to exchange information, support, and recipes (Bryant & Barnett, 2019; Ruby et al., 2018).

Intersectionality and social justice: Given the intersectionality of many oppressions, veganism has recently gotten entwined with larger social justice movements. By highlighting the links between animal rights, human rights, and environmental justice, activists have pushed for a more inclusive and egalitarian veganism that takes structural problems into account (Adams, 2010; Harper, 2018).

Technological advancements: Technological development has contributed to the development of veganism as well. The introduction of plant-based meat replacements like Beyond Meat and Impossible Foods has garnered interest and increased the alternatives available to people switching to a vegan diet. The distinction between conventional animal-based goods and their plant-based substitutes has become more hazy as a result of these advancements (Saxena, 2020; Sze et al., 2020). An important factor in the growth of vegan products is innovation. Companies are constantly looking for novel approaches to develop plant-based substitutes for traditional animal-derived goods that imitate their flavour, texture, and nutritional attributes. This includes the creation of new ingredients, sophisticated processing methods, and the blending of scientific discoveries and culinary knowledge. Inventive plant-based snacks, "bleeding" plant-based burgers, and dairy-free substitutes with rich flavours and creamy textures are just a few examples of the innovative advances being made in this field (Krzywonos & Piwowar, 2022).

6.2 THEORETICAL FOUNDATION

Veganism, a way of life that forgoes using animal products, has received a lot of attention in both academic and popular debate (Dagnelie, 2003). This review of the literature on veganism sought to examine significant themes and findings related to its ethical underpinnings, environmental effects, health effects, and social factors influencing its uptake (Ruby, 2012). The moral importance of animal welfare, cruelty-free behaviour, and the opposition to speciesism were emphasised by ethical arguments. Pimentel & Pimentel (2003) explored the ideas of sentience, moral concern, and the rights of non-human animals in order to assess the philosophical and moral arguments for veganism. Animal agriculture greatly increases greenhouse gas emissions, deforestation, and water pollution (Mottet, 2017).

Comparing diets that are based on animals and those that are plant-based reveals that switching to a vegan lifestyle might greatly lessen one's ecological impact. Numerous research studies have examined how a vegan diet compares to non-vegan diets in terms of its impact on health, which provide valuable insights into the potential health benefits associated with plant-based eating patterns (Tilman & Clark, 2014; Tuso et al., 2013).

According to research by Giaginis et al. (2023), a well-planned vegan diet can provide appropriate nutrition, including protein, vitamins, minerals, and vital fatty acids. Recent years have seen a rise in interest in studies examining the health benefits of veganism. Numerous studies have examined how well-nourished vegan dieters are and how their diets affect their health. The review looks at the potential advantages and drawbacks of a vegan diet, as well as the consumption of macronutrients, vitamins, minerals, and possible nutrient deficiency hazards. It also examines how going vegan can affect developing chronic conditions including cancer, diabetes, and heart disease (Dixon et al., 2023).

6.2.1 Veganism as a Sustainable Dietary Strategy

Vegans typically refer to veganism as a political philosophy based on the denial of the status of animals as commodities (Pedersen & Staescu, 2014) or as a component of an environmentally sustainable ideology (Buttny & Kinefuchi, 2020; Hudepohl, 2021). Although many people view being vegan as radical, it is progressively gaining popularity not only in Western societies but also in other cultures throughout the world (Forgrieve, 2018; Jones, 2020). However, the political, collective, and social movement facets of veganism receive little attention from academics. In order to comprehend and practice an environmentally sustainable way of life, it is crucial to have a broad grasp of veganism on an ideological and societal level.

Veganism is frequently seen as a sustainable eating plan due to its potential for having favourable environmental, ethical, and health effects. Veganism can help fight antibiotic resistance, which is a global health issue, by lowering the need for antibiotics in animal husbandry. Eliminating animal agriculture can boost the development of the plant-based food sector and advance sustainable economic growth (Leach et al., 2020).

6.2.2 Key reasons for Veganism as a Sustainable Choice

Reduced greenhouse gas emissions: Methane and nitrous oxide, in particular, are major greenhouse gas emissions which are associated with animal agriculture. Vegans often have a lower carbon footprint than non-vegans, which helps to slow down climate change (Judge et al., 2022).

Less deforestation: The development of animal husbandry frequently results in deforestation, which impedes the Earth's capacity to absorb carbon dioxide and also adds to habitat loss. Veganism encourages the preservation of forests (Tajfel &Turner, 1979).

Preservation of biodiversity: Intensive animal production frequently causes a decline in biodiversity. Vegans may safeguard endangered animals and maintain ecosystems by abstaining from animal products (Dhont et al., 2014).

Benefits for health: When balanced, a vegan diet can improve health and ease the strain on healthcare systems. By lowering healthcare expenses, this indirectly contributes to long-term sustainability (Cramer et al., 2017).

Innovation and alternative protein sources: Veganism has sparked research on lab-grown and plant-based meat substitutes that may provide sustainable solutions in the future by lowering the environmental effect of conventional meat production (Cruwys et al., 2020).

Impact on culture and the world: The popularity of veganism has encouraged more individuals to adopt sustainable eating practices on a global scale and change their food choices and behaviour (Buttny and Kinefuchi, 2020).

Although going vegan can be a sustainable dietary plan, the level of sustainability may differ depending on personal dietary preferences and the food's source. Not all vegan goods are made equal, and sustainability can still be impacted by different aspects like shipping, packaging, and farming methods. In the end, switching to a vegan diet is just one of the many possible alternatives people can take to lessen their impact on the environment and ethical issues. Choosing a sustainable diet and making broader efforts in agricultural and food systems can both be very helpful in tackling the problems associated with global sustainability (Drury et al., 2012). Veganism fosters the growth of more diverse and sustainable food systems that give priority to plant-based sources of nutrition by supporting a plant-based diet.

6.2.3 Challenges and Limitations of Vegan Products

However, there are also worries about the potential negative effects, such as potential nutritional gaps in specific life stages, limited food options in specific settings, and nutritional challenges. While a carefully planned vegan diet can satisfy nutritional requirements, poor planning or ignorance of healthy eating practices can lead to nutrient shortages, especially in vitamins B12, iron, calcium, and omega-3 fatty acids (Craig, 2009). In order to ensure optimal nutrient intake during specific life stages, such as pregnancy, lactation, infancy, or senior populations, additional consideration may be needed (Marsh et al., 2020). This may call for professional medical advice. Access to a wide variety of vegan food options may be restricted in some areas or in some circumstances, making it difficult for vegans to locate adequate selections when dining out or at particular social occasions.

Mayerfeld (2023) stated that adopting a vegan lifestyle may pose social challenges, including navigating social situations, dining out, and finding suitable options when traveling. Some individuals may face criticism, social stigma, or a lack of support from friends, family, or community. Nobari (2023) investigated that veganism is not a one-size-fits-all approach, and individuals have different dietary preferences, tastes, and cultural backgrounds. Adhering to a strict vegan diet may be challenging for some individuals, and they may choose to follow a more flexible or "flexitarian" approach instead. Limited nutritional education and guidance specific to vegan diets may pose a challenge for individuals seeking reliable information on meeting nutrient requirements and maintaining overall health while following a vegan lifestyle (Kothe et al., 2020; Melina et al., 2016).

6.3 RESEARCH METHODOLOGY

This research used NVivo 12 qualitative software to analyse secondary data. This chapter is split into three main sections; the first section entails the gathering of information (data, research papers, and other factors) in order to assess the effects of veganism on consumer health as well as to assess the various difficulties and restrictions for users. The analysis of veganism and vegan products' adoption, user perceptions, and insights are the main topics of the second phase. 17216 tweets were extracted and analysed using the NVivo software tool as part of the data collection for this phase, which was conducted on Twitter using the hashtag #vegan and #veganism up until May 1, 2023. The third phase extracted a CSV file with keywords as "vegan and veganism" from 1686 Scopus-published studies and examined the data to access the global public health opinion on veganism.

6.4 DATA ANALYSIS

The NVivo 12 qualitative software tool was used to evaluate the data that had been extracted. The investigation found that the users considered both the potential advantages and disadvantages of vegan products identifying a number of criteria.

6.4.1 Themes Identified through Twitter Analysis

Automated topic modeling and theme recognition from text-based datasets were made possible by the NVivo 12 software application. The primary topics that were extracted from the topic of veganism by the study using NVivo have included factors (displayed in Table 6.1) like social dynamics and family preferences, replicating the taste and texture of traditional chocolate, transition challenges for farmers, nutritional considerations, cultural- traditional significance as fur holds symbolic or historical value, and the use of fur may be deeply ingrained in their cultural practices.

This interpretation of thematic analysis explained that Twitter users focused on veganism especially in the context of "humane towards animals" followed by farms love and family concerns. The top eight themes are explained in Table 6.1. The consciousness towards the animal is inclining towards the changing choices towards the sustainable environment.

6.4.2 Sentimental Analysis in the Twitter Platform

In recent years, there has been a lot of research in the area of sentiment analysis on Twitter. At first, it concentrated on categorising opinions as either positive or negative on a binary scale. The extraction of up to four attitudes from text-based datasets is nevertheless possible with NVivo 12. Both written text and tweets can have their sentiment extracted using automated methods. Through the automated examination of vast volumes of data and the extraction of views, sentiment analysis can assist businesses and customers in achieving their objectives.

The sentiment analysis of individuals based on tweets is shown in Table 6.2. An increase has been observed in the positive and very positive perceptions of people towards veganism, which has gained importance in the recent past. By analysing the sentiment of

TABLE 6.1   Various Themes Identified under Veganism

S.no	Themes Identified	1: Files\\#Veganism –Twitter Search ~ Twitter
1	A: action	93
2	B: animal	71
3	C: chocolate	57
4	D: family	185
5	E: farm	251
6	F: food	77
7	G: fur	52
8	**H: humane towards animals**	**256**

TABLE 6.2   Sentiment Analysis through Twitter

	1: Files\\#vegan – Twitter Search ~ Twitter
A: Very negative	800
B: Moderately negative	720
C: Moderately positive	646
D: Very positive	212

FIGURE 6.1   Word cloud for Twitter analysis.

user responses to veganism or vegan products tweets, the major insights into the overall perception are shown; veganism has grown up to a total approximation of 36.1% as per Table 6.2, through Twitter analysis.

6.4.3 Word Cloud and World Map for Twitter Analysis

A technique called a word cloud creates a visual depiction of how frequently words and phrases were used. It is helpful for pinpointing important points to address when analysing data. In this study, tweets relating to veganism were examined using a word cloud. According to Figure 6.1, the word "Vegan" was in the word cloud's centre, surrounded by terms for organic foods and animal rights. This demonstrated that the main focus of the tweets was on animal welfare, cruelty-free practices and the rejection of specialism. The word map analysis of NVivo elicits that it has a wide range of users and applications and has been embraced by people and organisations across the world. This illustrated that vegan dietary choices are highly inclined towards animals and sustainable living culture. The majority of the opinions drawn on Twitter about veganism belong to the United

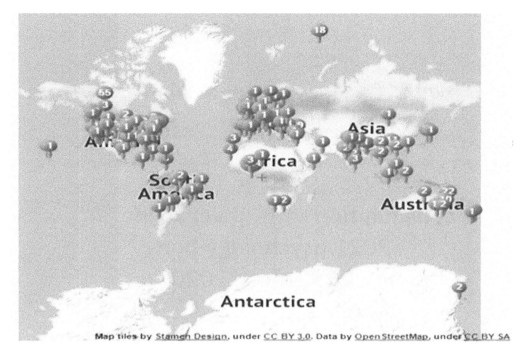

FIGURE 6.2   Word map in Twitter analysis.

TABLE 6.3   Thematic Analysis

Themes identified	Files\\#VeganismScopus data search
Food	1851
Study	1637
Diet	1436
Meat	1334
Vegan	1325
Eating	1224
Dietary	1022
Health	922
Consumption	920
Nutritional	919
Animal	918
Sustainable	915

States, Europe, the Middle East and South Asian countries, as per Figure 6.2, which clearly demonstrated that this is a worldwide phenomenon.

6.4.4 Thematic Analysis Using Scopus Data File

The third phase of this research paper focused on the Scopus-published study analysis. A CSV file is extracted from the Scopus database and exploratory research of thematic, sentimental and word cloud study has been conducted. Table 6.3 illustrates the twelve major areas of study in Scopus which highlighted "Vegan and Veganism" as keywords.

FIGURE 6.3   Word cloud for Scopus database study.

The study considered food, study, diet and meat as focus themes of the keywords identified. This demonstrated that the research papers conducted in the past on veganism are highly inclined to nutrition in diet, animal love and food as displayed in Table 6.3.

6.4.5 Word Cloud for Scopus Database

The word cloud analysis interpretation identified that the focus on veganism has increased majorly since 2018 and is inclined towards sustainable goals, nutritious food and responsibility towards animals. The Figure 6.3 word cloud has picked the most related words to be animal welfare, meat, health, environment and vegetarianism.

6.4.6 Sentiment Analysis for Scopus Database

The sentimental analysis in this exploratory study using NVivo of the Scopus database echoed the vegaphobic sentiments of the general public. Vegaphobia refers to the discrimination against vegans and vegetarians. The so-called meat dilemma can be used as one justification for vegaphobia. Many meat eaters dislike torturing animals. Maintaining bias against vegans can help meat eaters overcome this cognitive dissonance since vegans serve as a reminder of it. It's possible that vegans are not always vilified for ideological reasons. An upright interpretation of Figure 6.4 regards that approximately 36.3 per cent of the public is more conscious of holding a positive attitude towards veganism and health concerns and exhibiting their responsibility towards environmental concerns as per Figure 6.4.

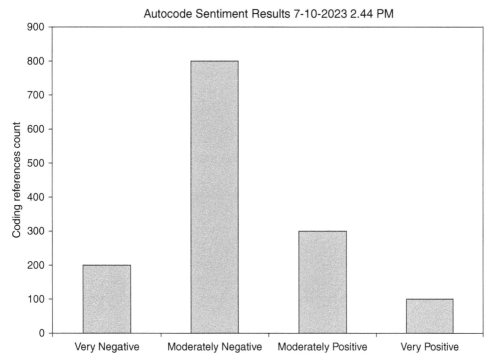

FIGURE 6.4   Sentimental analysis for Scopus database.

6.5 CONCLUSION

Veganism has become a global phenomenon. Although there aren't crowds of people waiting in line to become vegans, it has become more and more popular over the past ten years. Statistics from 2023 indicated that there are about 88 million vegans worldwide. Though it is a minute percentage of the population, a rising percentage declaring veganism is evoking a global trend supported by the world map analysis of Twitter data. India is a vast country with an almost 13 per cent vegan population followed by China and the United States with a three-quarters of women vegan population (Jen, 2023). This study emphasised the consumer insights of veganism by using NVivo software as a tool to visualise the consumer insights towards veganism. The Ncapture software study identified 17216 vegan-related tweets and recognised "vegan" as the ninth most trending topic worldwide, which illustrated the accepting phenomenon of veganism in the world. This study also considered 1686 exclusive Scopus research papers on veganism for qualitative analysis which can itself be considered as a huge slice of pie in consumer research of social sciences. This chapter conflated the analysis of sentimental, thematic analysis of Twitter social media; the Scopus database concluded the raising awareness of veganism. These results underlined the importance of vegan producers exploring new markets for consumer products in contrast to meat consumption.

REFERENCES

Adams, C. J. (1990). *The Sexual Politics of Meat: A Feminist-Vegetarian Critical Theory*. Bloomsbury Publishing.

Adams, C. J. (2010). *The Sexual Politics of Meat: A Feminist-Vegetarian Critical Theory*. Bloomsbury Publishing.

Aleksandrowicz, L., Green, R., Joy, E. J., Smith, P., & Haines, A. (2016). The impacts of dietary change on greenhouse gas emissions, land use, water use, and health: a systematic review. *PLoS One*, 11(11), e0165797.

Bhagat, S., & Ravi, S. S. (2018). Analysis of health drinks: What is satisfying consumer's thirst?. *Indian Journal of Marketing*, 48(9), 40–54.

Brown, M., & Jones, P., 2021. "Reducing environmental footprints: The role of vegan diets." *Sustainability*, 13(4), 210.

Bryant, C. J., & Barnett, J. C. (2019). Consumer behavior and marketing of vegan foods in the United Kingdom. *Foods*, 8(6), 251.

Buttny, R., & Kinefuchi, E. (2020). Vegans' problem stories: Negotiating vegan identity in dealing with omnivores. *Discourse &Society* 31, 565–583. DOI: 10.1177/0957926520939689

Craig, W. J. (2009). Health effects of vegan diets. *The American Journal of Clinical Nutrition*, 89(5), 1627S–1633S.

Craig, W. J., & Mangels, A. R. (2009). Position of the American dietetic association: Vegetarian diets. *Journal of the American Dietetic Association*, 109(7), 1266–1282.

Cramer, H., Kessler, C. S., Sundberg, T., Leach, M. J., Schumann, D., Adams, J., et al. (2017). Characteristics of Americans choosing vegetarian and vegan diets for health reasons. *Journal of Nutritional Education and Behavior* 49, 561–567.e1. DOI: 10.1016/j.jneb.2017.04.011

Cruwys, T., Norwood, R., Chachay, V. S., Ntontis, E., & Sheffield, J. (2020). "An important part of who I am": The predictors of dietary adherence among weightloss, vegetarian, vegan, paleo, and gluten-free dietary groups. *Nutrients* 12, 970. DOI: 10.3390/nu12040970

Dagnelie, P. C. (2003). Nutrition and health – the association between eating behavior and various health parameters: A Dutch longitudinal study. *Nutrition Journal*, 2(1), 9.

Dhont, K., Hodson, G., Costello, K., & MacInnis, C. C. (2014). Social dominance orientation connects prejudicial human–human and human–animal relations. *Personality and Individual Differences* 61–62, 105–108. DOI: 10.1016/j.paid.2013.12.020

Dinu, M., Abbate, R., Gensini, G. F., Casini, A., & Sofi, F. (2017). Vegetarian, vegan diets and multiple health outcomes: A systematic review with meta-analysis of observational studies. *Critical Reviews in Food Science and Nutrition*, 57(17), 3640–3649.

Dixon, K. A., Michelsen, M. K., & Carpenter, C. L. (2023). Modern diets and the health of our planet: An investigation into the environmental impacts of food choices. *Nutrients*, 15(3), 692.

Drury, J., Reicher, S., & Stott, C. (2012). "The psychology of collective action: Crowds and change," in *Culture and Social Change: Transforming Society Through Power of Ideas*, eds. B. Wagoner, E. Jensen, & J. Oldmeadow, Charlotte, NC: Information Age Publishing, 19–38.

Elsevier. (2021). Scopus. Retrieved from www.elsevier.com/solutions/scopus

Forgrieve, J. (2018). The growing acceptance of veganism. *Forbes*. Available online at: https://www.forbes.com/sites/janetforgrieve/2018/11/02/picturinga-kindler-gentler-world-vegan-month/?sh=5255983a2f2b (accessed July 22, 2021).

Fox, N., & Ward, K. (2008). Health, ethics and environment: A qualitative study of vegetarian motivations. *Appetite*, 50(2–3), 422–429.

Fresán, U., & Sabaté, J. (2019). Vegetarian diets: Planetary health and its alignment with human health. *Advances in Nutrition*, 10(4), S380–S388.

Giaginis, C., Mantzorou, M., Papadopoulou, S. K., Gialeli, M., Troumbis, A. Y., & Vasios, G. K. (2023). Christian orthodox fasting as a traditional diet with low content of refined carbohydrates that promotes human health: A review of the current clinical evidence. *Nutrients*, 15(5), 1225.

Harper, A. B. (2018). *Sistah Vegan: Black Female Vegans Speak on Food, Identity, Health, and Society*. Lantern Books.

Harrison, K., Vennard, D., & Madden, T. (2018). Exploring the commercialised Eden: The expansion of vegan markets. *Journal of Marketing Management*, 34(13–14), 1227–1250.

Huang, R. Y., Huang, C. C., Hu, F. B., & Chavarro, J. E. (2016). Vegetarian diets and weight reduction: A meta-analysis of randomized controlled trials. *Journal of General Internal Medicine*, 31(1), 109–116.

Hudepohl, D. (2021). Why going vegan is one of the best things you can do for the environment. *Forks Over Knives*. Available online at: https:// www.forksoverknives.com/wellness/vegan-diet-helps-environmentalsustainability/ (accessed August 04, 2021).

Jen Flatt Osborn. (2023, May29). How many vegans are in the world? Exploring the global population of vegans. World animal foundation. Retrived from https://worldanimalfoundation.org/advocate/how-many-vegans-are-in-the-world/#:~:text=According%20to%20Stats%20of%202023,world%2C%20that's%20around%201.1%25

Jones, L. (2020). Veganism: Why are vegan diets on the rise? BBC News. Available online at: www.bbc.com/news/business-44488051 (accessed August 04, 2021)

Judge, M., Fernando, J., & Begeny, C. (2022). Dietary behaviour as a form of collective action: A social identity model of vegan activism. *Appetite* 168, 105730. DOI: 10.1016/j.appet.2021.105730

Kothe, E. J., Mullan, B. A., & Butow, P. (2020). Promoting healthy eating and physical activity in adults: A review of multiple health behavior change interventions. *International Journal of Behavioral Nutrition and Physical Activity*, 17(1), 1–14.

Krzywonos, M., & Piwowar-Sulej, K. (2022). Plant-Based innovations for the transition to sustainability: A bibliometric and in-depth content analysis. *Foods*, 11(19), 3137.

Kwiatkowska, I., Olszak, J., Formanowicz, P., & Formanowicz, D. (2022). Nutritional status and habits among people on Vegan, Lacto/Ovo-Vegetarian, *Pescatarian and Traditional Diets*. *Nutrients*, 14(21), 4591.

Leach, S., Sutton, R. M., Dhont, K., & Douglas, K. M. (2020). When is it wrong to eat animals? The relevance of different animal traits and behaviors. *European Journal of Social Psychology* 51, 113–123. DOI: 10.1002/ejsp.2718

Marsh, K. A., Munn, E. A., Baines, S. K., Smith, M., Long, S., & Milross, C. G. (2020). Health implications of a vegan diet: A review. *Nutrients*, 12(11), 3400.

Mayerfeld, D. (2023). The limits of vegetarianism. In *Our Carbon Hoofprint: The Complex Relationship Between Meat and Climate*. Cham: Springer International Publishing, 57–83.

Melina, V., Craig, W., & Levin, S. (2016). Position of the academy of nutrition and dietetics: Vegetarian diets. *Journal of the Academy of Nutrition and Dietetics*, 116(12), 1970–1980.

Miller, A. (2022). The growing trend of veganism: A comprehensive analysis. *Journal of Social and Cultural Studies*, 40(3), 315–330.

Mintel. (2021). Plant-based Proteins – US – February 2021. Retrieved from https://store.mintel.com/report/plant-based-proteins-us-february-2021

Mottet, A., de Haan, C., Falcucci, A., Tempio, G., Opio, C., & Gerber, P. (2017). Livestock: On our plates or eating at our table? A new analysis of the feed/food debate. *Global food security*, 14, 1–8.

Nobari, N. (2023). Meet the new vegan world. In *Oppressive Liberation: Sexism in Animal Activism*. Cham: Springer International Publishing, 275–287

Pedersen, H., & Staescu, V. (2014). "Conclusion: Future directions for critical animal studies," in *The Rise of Critical Animal Studies: From the Margins to Centre*, eds. N. Taylor & R. Twine, New York: Routledge, 262–276

Pimentel, D., & Pimentel, M. (2003). Sustainability of meat-based and plant-based diets and the environment. *The American Journal of Clinical Nutrition*, 78(3), 660S–663S.

QSR International. (2021). NVivo: Qualitative data analysis software. Retrieved from www.qsrinternational.com/nvivo-qualitative-data-analysis-software

Ruby, M. B. (2012). Vegetarianism. A blossoming field of study. *Appetite*, 58(1), 141–150.

Ruby, M. B., Heine, S. J., Kamble, S., Cheng, T. K., & Waddar, M. (2018). Compassion and contamination. Cultural differences in vegetarianism. *Appetite*, 71, 340–348.

Saxena, J. (2020). Plant-Based meat alternatives: Benefits, challenges, and opportunities. *Foods*, 9(5), 686.

Scarborough, P., Appleby, P. N., Mizdrak, A., Briggs, A. D., Travis, R. C., Bradbury, K. E., & Key, T. J. (2014). Dietary greenhouse gas emissions of meat-eaters, fish-eaters, vegetarians and vegans in the UK. *Climatic Change*, 125(2), 179–192.

Singer, P. (1975). *Animal Liberation*. HarperCollins.

Smith, J., 2020. "The surge in Veganism: Trends and implications." *Environmental Ethics*, 48(3), 315–330.

Sze, Y. Y., Zhou, Y., Wallin, S., & Shepon, A. (2020). The role of plant-based diets in sustainable global food security. *Global Food Security*, 26, 100410.

Tajfel, H., & Turner, J. C. (1979). An integrative theory of intergroup conflict. In *The Social Psychology of Intergroup Relations*, eds. W. G. Austin & S. Worchel, Monterey, CA: Brooks, Cole Pub, p. 33–47.

Tilman, D., & Clark, M. (2014). Global diets link environmental sustainability and human health. *Nature*, 515(7528), 518–522.Tuso, P. J., Ismail, M. H., Ha, B. P., & Bartolotto, C. (2013). Nutritional update for physicians: Plant-based diets. *The Permanente Journal*, 17(2), 61–66.

Tuso, P. J., Ismail, M. H., Ha, B. P., & Bartolotto, C. (2013). Nutritional update for physicians: Plant-based diets. *The Permanente Journal*, 17(2), 61–66.

Twitter. (2021). About twitter. Retrieved from https://about.twitter.com/

Watson, D. (1945). Nutrition and ethical aspects of the vegan diet. *Journal of Home Economics*, 37(6), 513–519.

CHAPTER 7

Monitoring of Water Toxicity Through the Internet of Things to Protect the Health of the Population

Khadija El-Moustaqim, Jamal Mabrouki
and Mourade Azrour

7.1 INTRODUCTION

Water is much more than a simple human need. It represents an essential and irreplaceable element to ensure the continuity of life[1]. However, it can also be a source of disease. According to the literature, millions of infants and children die each year from diseases caused by contaminated food or drinking water. Drinking water is a key factor in the prevention of water-related diseases and should be given special attention. Indeed, water intended for human consumption must not contain dangerous chemical substances, or pathogenic germs harmful to health[2]. This is why all the actors in the water sector must constantly monitor the quality of the groundwater resource, which conditions the safety and reliability of the drinking water supply for the population, and continue to recover the quality of surface water in each agglomeration[3]–[8]. Also, the use of water from public open wells and unprotected individual wells, combined with the inadequacy of sanitation facilities and ignorance of basic hygiene rules, promotes the spread of diseases Oro-fecal transmission and can cause serious diseases such as gastroenteritis, hepatitis, and typhoid. The rapid increase in the population produces a large amount of wastewater, contaminating rivers, ponds, and reservoirs and making freshwater a limited and valuable resource. As well as climate change, depletion of ecosystems, inappropriate use of renewable capital, and also ecological stresses are inseparably linked to the reduction of rivers due to low groundwater flow[3], [9]. In addition, this deteriorates the reservoirs, which has a negative effect on the supply and availability of water.

DOI: 10.1201/9781003430735-7

In this paper, we present a general study on the use of the Internet of Things (IoT) in monitoring systems for the detection of several particles in wastewater. In the second part of this paper, we will approach a study in the form of a literature review on the evolution of different techniques used in IoT-based monitoring systems to detect various materials. All we discuss are their main properties and their potential.

7.2 IOT AND WASTEWATER

In recent years, the technology sector has undergone a real evolution. Moreover, it has become an indispensable tool in our daily life. Among these recent technologies, IoT has been continuously improved and has attracted more and more people. This growth has had a positive impact on many sectors, including home security, smart grids, etc. [10]–[15]. As a result, the number of connected devices is increasing day by day. As a type of wireless sensor network using technology for water quality monitoring and management, the use of wireless sensors on IoT network installations improves on current centralized systems and traditional manual methods, allowing the distributed intelligent water quality system to adapt to urban dynamics and heterogeneous water distribution infrastructures[16]–[20]. IoT refers to a new wide area network that allows any object to be connected to the internet in order to exchange data and be controlled remotely. This communication technology is used to transfer data from a physical entity to a device with intelligent analysis tools through a wireless channel[21], which is designed to improve the protection and quality of wastewater treatment. IoT relies on connecting the physical environment to the internet for the purpose of monitoring and managing wastewater. IoT technologies are implemented with sensors to monitor water in connected environments. Water monitoring using IoT can overcome key barriers to effective water management[22]–[24]. Traditional monitoring techniques can satisfy water use, efficiency, quantitative detection, and treatment. Therefore, storage and circumstance indicators can be established in sewage and wastewater treatment plants. In addition, it effectively controls wireless connectivity and remote monitoring of water strains, contaminants, water data, land use, resources, and drains. IoT water management has a huge capacity to provide massive processing options; environmental, structural, and ecological attributes of various forms of media[25], [26]. Thus, it has a catalytic effect on creativity to incorporate the main decision of sensing technologies, including sensors, remote sensing, and others, and would have the advantage of controlling the commentary on the performance of water by developing new technologies to protect the human input.

To better understand the architecture of the IoT (Figure 7.1), one of its essential requirements is that the objects in the network must be connected to each other. That guarantees IoT system architecture operation, which connects the physical and virtual worlds. When designing the IoT architecture, scalability, extensibility, and operability of devices should be considered.

The existing IoT architecture can be used for wastewater management but is better suited for consumer applications, where the risk impact factor is low. The IoT can facilitate

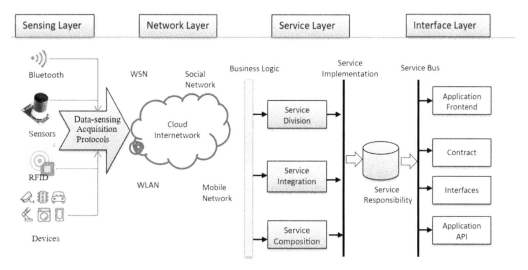

FIGURE 7.1   Architectural layers of IoT.

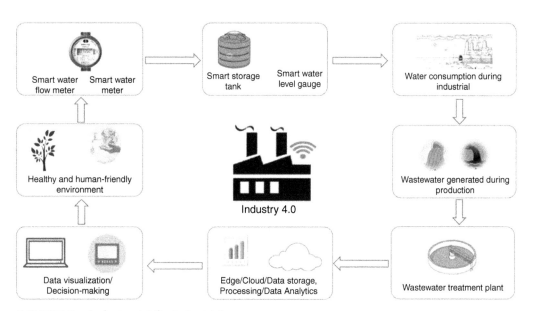

FIGURE 7.2   Industry 4.0 for industrial wastewater management.

the accurate evolution of many transactions, lead to better industrial waste management, and help track the waste stream without the risk of data tampering (Figure 7.2).

7.3 THE EFFECTS OF TOXIC CHEMICALS

The development of our societies has led to increased production of potentially toxic chemical molecules, spilled accidentally or not into the environment. As early as the 1930s, a link between air pollution and respiratory pathologies was established, but it was not until the early 1950s that the first scientific reports on the chemical contamination of

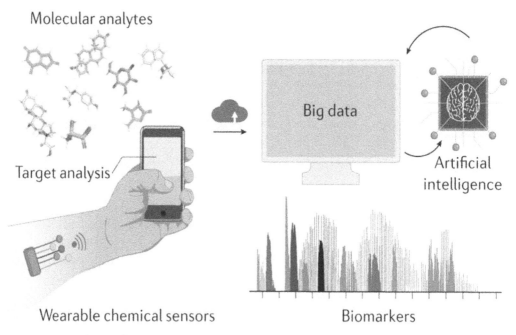

Molecular analytes

Target analysis

Big data

Artificial intelligence

Wearable chemical sensors

Biomarkers

FIGURE 7.3   Chemical sensor array.

food appeared. The contamination of food revealed by frequent health scandals awakens an increased vigilance of populations and health authorities. The toxicity of many food contaminants on human cells and organs is now better documented[27]–[29]. The toxic effects of chemical contaminants on marine organisms depend on bioavailability and persistence, the ability of organisms to accumulate and metabolize contaminants, and the interference of contaminants with ecological, metabolic or specific processes. A wide range of toxicity tests has been developed in recent years to allow rapid and accurate screening for the toxic effects of chemicals (Figure 7.3). Toxicity is also found in plastics that are rarely biodegradable. They are usually fragmented into huge quantities of macro, micro, and nanoparticles by different processes and in natural conditions, which makes them ubiquitous and dangerous pollutants for the environment worldwide[30].

7.4 THE EVOLUTION OF WATER BIOSENSING TECHNIQUES

L. Campanella et al.[31] proposed an algal biosensor for the evolution of toxicity in estuarine waters. The sensor was obtained by coupling an adapted algal bioreceptor (the cyanobacterium spirulina subsalsa) to an amperometric electrode with a gas diffusion. The analysis that was done allowed us to follow the evolution of photosynthetic O_2 and the detection of alterations due to toxic effects caused by environmental pollutants present in the environment. Four chemical species representatives of three main classes of pollutants (heavy metals, triazine herbicides, carbamate insecticides) were tested at different concentrations using standardized natural water as an experimental medium. In all cases, a toxic response was detected; that is, a dose-related inhibition of photosynthetic activity was recorded with good reproducibility. The automated system developed in this study monitored the photosynthetic activity of an appropriate bioreceptor in the absence and pre of toxic agents, recording the oxygen produced with a lifetime of at least two days. In the presence of toxic agents, reproducible dose-dependent responses were detected. The proposed biosensor was highly sensitive to atrazine and showed intermediate sensitization to carbaryl, while toxicity detection in the case of heavy metals was slow. This could be due to biological factors related to the adsorption characteristics of the cell walls as well as the specific sequestration, metabolization, and release pathways of the algal species used.

The online water quality management system (OWQMS), as proposed by Shumei Wang et al.[32] is one of the main components of the environmental Internet of Things (IoT), including an online water quality monitoring subsystem, by implementing a digital data transmission subsystem and data processing elements, to manage an urban tourist river. Including the input of reclaimed domestic wastewater and fresh surface water from the Xinglin channel to maintain the water level of the river, and the water cycle of the landscape to stabilize the water quality that was examined. Then they showed that no water deterioration was detected throughout the period, and it was proved that the OWQMS system was effective in managing the scenic river and maintaining the water quality of the landscape stable over the past four years. The treatment performance showed results that suggest that the campus wastewater treatment plant was effective in degrading organic carbon, and for ammonia nitrogen, due to mixing with the laboratory wastewater, the influent was kept relatively low with the wastewater and a relatively low concentration in the range of 1.27–12.33 mg L^{-1}. This allows the authors to find that the OWQMS system was effective in managing the scenic river and maintaining stable water quality. Strong self-purification in the water body on pollutants, especially nitrogen and phosphate degradation, was observed, while water deterioration was not detected throughout the period. The reclaimed wastewater should be treated in the wetland before being observed in the campus river. The results are shown after treatment in the wetland. Various water quality parameters reached the standard demand, which suggests that the recycling of river water is an effective way to stabilize the quality of the river in the future.

Due to the population growth, urbanization of rural areas, and excessive use of marine resources for salt extraction, the depletion of water resources becomes critical, prompting Varcha Lakchmikantha et al.[33] to propose an intelligent system to monitor water quality. This system is composed of sensors that allow measuring the values in real-time, accompanied by an Arduino ATMEGA 328 software that can convert the analog values to digital values with an LCD screen that displays the outputs of the sensors. The connection was ensured by the Wi-Fi module between the hardware and the software. They showed that after testing the three water samples and depending on their results, they were able to classify the water as potable or not, hence they recommended the use of these sensors in order to detect various quality parameters, use wireless communication standards for better communication and IoT to create a better monitoring system in the reason of making safe by an immediate response.

Marielle Thomas presented in her research thesis a new biological detection process. Its principle is based on the automatic characterization of electrical signals by a tropical fish. This work dealt with the influence of several physicochemical parameters (temperature, pH, conductivity, and dissolved oxygen) on the characteristics of the studied material concerning six polluting substances. The implementation of this new process allowed the detection in less than 35 minutes[34].

7.5 CONCLUSION

The current research is based on water pollution, which is treated as a high threat to the world, as it affects health and the economy and spoils biodiversity. So, in this work, the causes and effects of water pollution are all discussed based on a literature review of works that have adopted different water monitoring techniques, and which are IoT-based methods for water quality have been addressed. Although there have been many excellent smart water quality monitoring systems, the research area is still challenging. This work presents examples of recent work done by researchers to make water quality monitoring systems intelligent and also that can be more effective for detecting water toxicity. These systems are characterized by low power, so monitoring is continuous, and alerts/notifications are sent to the concerned authorities for further processing. These systems have shown high efficiency for water detection.

REFERENCES

[1] M. Azrour, J. Mabrouki, G. Fattah, A. Guezzaz, et F. Aziz, Machine learning algorithms for efficient water quality prediction, *Model. Earth Syst. Environ.*, vol. 8, n° 2, p. 2793–2801, 2022.

[2] J. Mabrouki, M. Azrour, et S. E. Hajjaji, Use of internet of things for monitoring and evaluating water's quality: A comparative study, *Int. J. Cloud Comput.*, vol. 10, n° 5–6, p. 633–644, 2021.

[3] T. X. Bien, A. Jaafari, T. Van Phong, P. T. Trinh, et B. T. Pham, Groundwater potential mapping in the central highlands of Vietnam using spatially explicit machine learning, *Earth Sci. Inform.*, vol. 16, p. 131–146, 2023.

[4] H. E. Elzain *et al.*, Novel machine learning algorithms to predict the groundwater vulnerability index to nitrate pollution at two levels of modeling, *Chemosphere*, vol. 314, p. 137671, 2023.

[5] M. Azrour, J. Mabrouki, A. Guezzaz, S. Benkirane, and H. Asri, Implementation of Real-Time Water Quality Monitoring Based on Java and Internet of Things, in *Integrating Blockchain and Artificial Intelligence for Industry 4.0 Innovations*, S. Goundar and R. Anandan, Eds., in EAI/Springer Innovations in Communication and Computing. Cham: Springer International Publishing, 2024, pp. 133–143. DOI: 10.1007/978-3-031-35751-0_8

[6] N. Jineshkumar, U. Krishnan, et T. Kalavathi Devi, Estimation of water quality using wireless sensor networks, *Int. J. Res. Appl. Sci. Eng. Technol.*, vol. 6, n° 2, p. 1101–1106, 2018.

[7] Z. Zhang, J. Huang, S. Duan, Y. Huang, J. Cai, et J. Bian, Use of interpretable machine learning to identify the factors influencing the nonlinear linkage between land use and

river water quality in the Chesapeake Bay watershed, *Ecol. Indic.*, vol. 140, p. 108977, juill. 2022. DOI: 10.1016/j.ecolind.2022.108977

[8] L. Zhang, M. He, W. Hu, et H. Ge, Machine learning and first-principles insights on molecularly modified CH3NH3PbI3 film in water, *Appl. Surf. Sci.*, vol. 593, p. 153428, août 2022. DOI: 10.1016/j.apsusc.2022.153428

[9] D. Singh et V. Sharma, Review of groundwater potential storage and recharge zone map delineation using statistics based hydrological and machine learning based artificial intelligent models, in *2023 Somaiya International Conference on Technology and Information Management (SICTIM)*, IEEE, 2023, p. 6–11.

[10] H. Attou, M. Mohy-Eddine, A. Guezzaz *et al.*, Towards an intelligent intrusion detection system to detect malicious activities in cloud computing, *Appl. Sci.,* vol. 13, no. 17, p. 9588, 2023.

[11] M. Mohy-eddine, A. Guezzaz, S. Benkirane, et M. Azrour, IoT-Enabled smart agriculture: Security issues and applications, in *Artificial Intelligence and Smart Environment: ICAISE'2022*, Springer, 2023, p. 566–571.

[12] C. Hazman, S. Benkirane, A. Guezzaz, M. Azrour, et M. Abdedaime, Intrusion detection framework for IoT-Based smart environments security, in *Artificial Intelligence and Smart Environment: ICAISE'2022*, Springer, 2023, p. 546–552.

[13] C. Hazman, A. Guezzaz, S. Benkirane, et M. Azrour, lIDS-SIoEL: Intrusion detection framework for IoT-based smart environments security using ensemble learning, *Clust. Comput.*, p. 1–15, 2022.

[14] G. Fattah, J. Mabrouki, F. Ghrissi, M. Azrour, et Y. Abrouki, Multi-Sensor system and internet of things (IoT) technologies for air pollution monitoring, in *Futuristic Research Trends and Applications of Internet of Things*, CRC Press, 2022.

[15] M. Azrour, J. Mabrouki, A. Guezzaz, et A. Kanwal, Internet of things security: Challenges and key issues, *Secur. Commun. Netw.*, vol. 2021, p. 1–11, sept. 2021. doi: 10.1155/2021/5533843

[16] K. S. Adu-Manu, F. A. Katsriku, J.-D. Abdulai, et F. Engmann, Smart river monitoring using wireless sensor networks, *Wirel. Commun. Mob. Comput.*, vol. 2020, p. e8897126, sept. 2020. DOI: 10.1155/2020/8897126

[17] T. Anuradha, Bhakti, R. Chaitra, et D. Pooja, IoT Based Llw cost system for monitoring of water quality in real time, *Int. Res. J. Eng. Technol. IRJET*, vol. 5, n° 5, p. 1658–1663, mai 2018.

[18] J. Mabrouki, A. El Yadini, I. Bencheikh, K. Azoulay, A. Moufti, et S. El Hajjaji, Hydrogeological and hydrochemical study of underground waters of the tablecloth in the vicinity of the controlled city dump mohammedia (Morocco), in *Advanced Intelligent Systems for Sustainable Development (AI2SD'2018)* Vol 3: Advanced Intelligent Systems Applied to Environment, Springer, 2019, p. 22–33.

[19] J. Mabrouki *et al.*, Geographic information system for the study of water resources in Chaâba El Hamra, Mohammedia (Morocco), in *Artificial Intelligence and Smart Environment: ICAISE'2022*, Springer, 2023, p. 469–474.

[20] M. Mohy-Eddine, M. Azrour, J. Mabrouki, F. Amounas, A. Guezzaz, et S. Benkirane, Embedded web server implementation for real-time water monitoring, in *Advanced Technology for Smart Environment and Energy*, J. Mabrouki, A. Mourade, A. Irshad, et S. A. Chaudhry, Éd., in Environmental Science and Engineering. Cham: Springer International Publishing, 2023, p. 301–311. DOI: 10.1007/978-3-031-25662-2_24

[21] Y. Li, G. Huang, Y. Huang, et X. Qin, Modeling of water quality, quantity, and sustainability, *J. Appl. Math.*, vol. 2014, p. e135905, août 2014 DOI: 10.1155/2014/135905

[22] A. N. Afif, F. Noviyanto, S. Sunardi, S. A. Akbar, et E. Aribowo, Integrated application for automatic schedule-based distribution and monitoring of irrigation by applying the waterfall model process, *Bull. Electr. Eng. Inform.*, vol. 9, nº 1, févr. 2020. DOI: 10.11591/eei.v9i1.1368

[23] T. Dang et J. Liu, Design of water quality monitoring system in Shaanxi section of Weihe river basin based on the internet of things, *Comput. Intell. Neurosci.*, vol. 2022, p. e3543937, juill. 2022. DOI: 10.1155/2022/3543937

[24] D. Li et S. Liu, Water Quality Evaluation, in *Water Quality Monitoring and Management*, Elsevier, 2019, p. 113–159. DOI: 10.1016/B978-0-12-811330-1.00004-1

[25] S. A. H. AlMetwally, M. K. Hassan, et M. H. Mourad, Real time internet of things (IoT) based water quality management system, *Procedia CIRP*, vol. 91, p. 478–485, 2020. DOI: 10.1016/j.procir.2020.03.107

[26] R. Ullah *et al.*, EEWMP: An IoT-Based Energy-Efficient water management platform for smart irrigation, *Sci. Program.*, vol. 2021, p. e5536884, avr. 2021. DOI: 10.1155/2021/5536884

[27] M. Boukandou Mounanga, L. Mewono, et S. Aboughe Angone, Toxicity studies of medicinal plants used in sub-Saharan Africa, *J. Ethnopharmacol.*, vol. 174, p. 618–627, nov. 2015. DOI: 10.1016/j.jep.2015.06.005

[28] I. Saadi, Y. Laor, M. Raviv, et S. Medina, Land spreading of olive mill wastewater: Effects on soil microbial activity and potential phytotoxicity, *Chemosphere*, vol. 66, nº 1, p. 75–83, janv. 2007. DOI: 10.1016/j.chemosphere.2006.05.019

[29] R. Altenburger *et al.*, Future water quality monitoring: Improving the balance between exposure and toxicity assessments of real-world pollutant mixtures, *Environ. Sci. Eur.*, vol. 31, nº 1, p. 12, févr. 2019. DOI: 10.1186/s12302-019-0193-1

[30] W. Zhang, Q. X. Liu, Z. H. Guo, et J. S. Lin, Practical application of aptamer-based biosensors in detection of low molecular weight pollutants in water sources, *Molecules*, vol. 23, nº 2, p. 344, 2018.

[31] L. Campanella, F. Cubadda, M. P. Sammartino, et A. Saoncella, An algal biosensor for the monitoring of water toxicity in estuarine environments, *Water Res.*, vol. 35, nº 1, p. 69–76, janv. 2001. DOI: 10.1016/S0043-1354(00)00223-2

[32] S. Wang, Z. Zhang, Z. Ye, X. Wang, X. Lin, et S. Chen, Application of environmental internet of things on water quality management of urban scenic river, *Int. J. Sustain. Dev. World Ecol.*, vol. 20, nº 3, p. 216–222. juin 2013. DOI: 10.1080/13504509.2013.785040

[33] V. Lakshmikantha, A. Hiriyannagowda, A. Manjunath, A. Patted, J. Basavaiah, et A. A. Anthony, IoT based smart water quality monitoring system, *Glob. Transit. Proc.*, vol. 2, no 2, p. 181–186, nov. 2021. DOI: 10.1016/j.gltp.2021.08.062

[34] V. Lakshmikantha, A. Hiriyannagowda, A. Manjunath, A. Patted, J. Basavaiah, et A. A. Anthony, IoT based smart water quality monitoring system, Glob. Transit. Proc., vol. 2, no 2, p. 181–186, nov. 2021. DOI: 10.1016/j.gltp.2021.08.062

Index

A

access control 59, 61, 63, 66
air pollution 27, 87
arduino 89
artificial intelligence 13, 14, 16, 18, 19, 42, 44, 46, 48, 50, 51, 62, 63, 66
authentication 57–61, 64, 66

B

behavioral traits 62
big data 5, 37, 57
bioavailability 88
biomarker 26, 31, 33, 34, 36, 62
biometric data 5, 57–9, 62, 63, 65, 66
biometric monitoring 60
biopsy 27
bitcoin 1, 2
blood 26, 48, 59, 60, 63–5

C

cancer 13, 15, 19, 25–38
chemical substance 85
chest radiography 26
chronic disease 14, 46, 62, 64
classification 3, 4, 16, 26–31, 33, 37
clinical 8, 13, 14, 16, 19, 34, 44, 48, 49, 51, 65, 66
cloud 2, 3, 6, 34, 37, 78, 80
computed tomography 26
confidentiality 1, 46, 47, 63
contaminated food 85
contamination 87, 88
coronavirus 1
cytopathological 26

D

dangerous 85, 88
data security 3, 6, 18, 19, 38, 47, 62, 63, 64

decision-making 13, 18, 19, 29, 34, 43, 49, 51
development 1, 2, 5, 7, 16, 18, 43, 45, 49–51, 73–5, 87
diagnoses 13, 15, 18, 26, 27, 43, 44, 45, 51
diagnosis 1, 2, 14–16, 26, 27, 31, 33, 38, 43–5, 49–51, 60, 61, 63
DNA 26, 31
doctor 6, 8, 19, 38, 43, 45, 47, 51, 58, 60–3
drinking water 85
drug 13–18, 43, 47, 51, 52, 59, 61, 63, 64

E

eating disorders 13
ecological 74, 85, 86, 88
e-health 64, 66
environment 43, 44, 46, 50, 64, 71–3, 77, 80, 86–9
ethereum 1

F

facial recognition 58, 60, 62, 66
farming 72, 76
fingerprint 57, 59, 61, 62, 64, 66

G

genetic data 49, 64
greenhouse 73
groundwater 85

H

health authorities 88
health records 3, 14, 16, 49, 50, 59, 61, 64
healthcare organizations 2, 6, 50, 60–3
heart disease 13, 47, 62, 71–4
heart rate variability 60
histopathology 27
hospital 2, 6, 16, 18, 19, 36, 42, 44, 46, 48, 61, 63
hyperledger 1

I

industry 4.0 87
intelligent decisions 13
Internet of Medical Things 5
Internet of Things 1, 42, 57, 63, 66, 85, 86, 89
iris 57–62, 64

K

K-nearest neighbors 29, 33, 36

L

lifestyle 5, 43, 46–8, 64, 65, 71, 73, 74, 76
lung cancer 19, 25–35

M

map 78, 79, 81
meat consumption 81
medical errors 14, 57, 59, 61
medical image 6, 14, 18, 19, 30, 45
medicine 7, 14–18, 20, 30, 47, 51, 52, 58, 59, 63
metabolic 26, 34, 88
misdiagnosis 61

N

naive bayes 29, 34
national economic 1
neural network 25–7, 32–4, 36, 37

P

particularly diabetes 13
pathologies 2, 12, 25, 28
patient 13, 14, 16, 18, 19, 34, 36, 38, 42–5, 48, 51, 57, 58, 60–5
patient identification 57–61, 64, 66
patient identity 61, 62, 65
policies 1, 62
predictive analytics 42, 44–6, 67, 51
preprocessing 28–31
privacy 1–3, 17–19, 38, 43, 46, 47, 50, 51, 61–3, 65, 66

R

random forest 29, 32–4, 36
real-time 6, 58, 62, 89
remote monitoring 44, 48, 58, 86

remote sensing 86
retina scans 60
robotic 44, 48, 49

S

security 1–3, 5, 17, 19, 38, 47, 58, 59, 61–4, 66, 86
sensors 5, 16, 48, 49, 58, 59, 60, 63, 64, 89
sentiment analysis 77, 80
smoking 25, 27
speech analysis 60
stress 60, 85
support vector machines 29, 31–3, 36, 38
surgical 30, 48, 49

T

technology 1–3, 5, 6, 31, 42, 44–6, 49–51, 58, 60, 62, 64, 67
telemedicine 43, 44, 58, 64, 66
tobacco 25
toxic 87–9
toxicity 85, 88–90
traditional healthcare 2, 46
trustworthy 18, 61
tumor 26, 28, 31, 32, 34, 35, 38, 45
twitter 72, 76–8, 81

U

unauthorized access 50, 57, 58, 61–3

V

veganism 71, 73–8, 80, 81
vigilance 88
voice recognition 60
vulnerable 5, 62

W

wastewater 85–7, 89
water pollution 73, 74, 90
water quality 86, 89, 90
wearable device 58, 59, 66
wireless 86

X

XGBoost Tree 30
X-ray 14, 16, 19, 43, 45